IMAGES
of America

CRANFORD
VOLUME II

ON THE RIVER. Cranford is a river town. It was the river that attracted the first settlers here, and it was the river that drew the New Yorkers and Brooklynites who established the township in 1871. This scene shows the unique three-horse stable behind the Moore house (built 1862) at 22 Central Avenue, owned today by James Lenny. The stable features fish-scale shingles and dressed-stone, brick, cobblestone, and fieldstone walls. (Photograph by Greg Price.)

IMAGES
of America

CRANFORD
VOLUME II

Robert Fridlington and Lawrence Fuhro

ARCADIA

First published 1996
Copyright © Robert Fridlington and Lawrence Fuhro, 1996

ISBN 0-7524-0477-6

Published by Arcadia Publishing,
an imprint of the Chalford Publishing Corporation
One Washington Center, Dover, New Hampshire 03820
Printed in Great Britain

Library of Congress Cataloging-in-Publication Data applied for

This book is affectionately dedicated to the memory of
Arthur and Hazel Burditt.

Contents

CRANE'S FORD TABLET. One of the more familiar monuments in Cranford is the boulder and tablet found at the junction of Normandie Place and Riverside Drive, just a few feet from Springfield Avenue and Memorial Park. The tablet was erected by the Cranford Historical Society on July 4, 1929, to mark the site of Crane's Ford, the traditional low-water crossing on the Rahway River. Modern historians question the story cited on the tablet that "here light horsemen guarded while General Washington's army was encamped at Morristown."

Introduction

In 1995 we brought out Images of America: *Cranford*, a collection of photographs that was our salute to Cranford's 125th anniversary. In that volume, we showed some of the people, places, and events that had contributed to the color and substance of the township's past. The reception given to that book by the community exceeded our fondest expectations. It was apparent that many natives of Cranford maintained an exceptionally strong attachment to the community. Requests for the book came from all over the United States, many of them containing reminiscences of Cranford in years gone by. At the same time, many newcomers and relatively short-term residents expressed their delight in learning more about the township's history. One of the most rewarding reactions to the book has come from young people. It has found a place in the schools, from show-and-tell activities to high school history classes, and it has been used as the basis for guided tours of the township. If in this volume we have emphasized personalities a little more than previously, it is because we believe that the town's strength and its history rest with its people. This is not a typical picture history. We present it, like its predecessor, as a Cranford family album, and we hope the family members will enjoy it.

Robert Fridlington and Lawrence Fuhro
September 1996

Acknowledgments

This book would not be what it is without the help of many people. We are grateful to the trustees of the Cranford Historical Society who again permitted us to use photographs from the society's collection. For permission to use the photograph on p. 2, we are indebted to Greg Price. Fred Crenshaw, Philomena Dalessandris, Ira Dorian, Alfred Fricke, Robert Greco, Lillian Jones, Wesley Philo, and Vincent Sarnowski lent us pictures and provided information. John E. Allen, Clark Duckworth, Betty Hansel, Angelo Illuminati, Phyllis Rabino, and Adelaide Weil gave invaluable assistance, often on short notice. To all of these friends we are grateful.

A special thanks goes to Linda Keller and Bonnie Goldstein of the Reference Department of the Cranford Public Library for their cheerful and efficient assistance. Mere acknowledgement cannot repay the debt owed to the large and mostly anonymous group of photographers who captured these special moments on film.

And last, we say thanks to Joan Fridlington and Laura Fuhro who bore it all with patience, good humor, and understanding.

"And when I go—as go I must—still others will rise up to trudge along the highway of the past. Only such as I may smile at them. Will you?"
— I.B. Herodotus (William Bragdon) in his last "Do You Remember" column, *Cranford Citizen and Chronicle*, February 9, 1933.

One
From Farm Village to Suburb
1871-1889

THE HOME OF A CRANE, ABOUT 1871. This tattered photograph shows the home of Josiah Crane Jr., about the time Cranford incorporated. Josiah Jr. was one of the original incorporators of the township. Said to have been built in 1767, the house stood near the northwest corner of Springfield and North Union Avenues. From the 1880s until it was razed in 1903, the house was the residence of the Bookhout family. The tree in the picture stands today in the parking lot of the Gray Memorial Funeral Home. It is the sole survivor of the homestead around which the township grew up.

The Cranford Times.

A MONTHLY AMATEUR PAPER DEVOTED TO TOWN NEWS, EDITORIALS, POETRY, SHORT STORIES, &C.

VOL. II.	NOVEMBER, 1872.	No. 7.

PROBABLE CANDIDATES FOR THE COMING SPRING ELECTION

EXCITING TIMES EXPECTED.

The property holders, citizens, and in fact every one in town have started to discuss and criticise our "arrogant" township officials. The people are going to have a "PEOPLES' TICKET" at the next election, with good, clean candidates upon it irrespective of politics. We feel very sure that the following named gentlemen will be the nominees on the ticket:—

Freeholder, Thomas Cloyd,
Town Clerk, Wm. R. Christmas,
Town Committee, A. P. Purves,
"   "   John W. Close,
"   "   E. K. Adams,
"   "   E. S. Crane,
"   "   Jacob Ludlow,
Road Board, J. K. Miller,
Assessor, Gideon E. Ludlow,
Collector, Moses T. Crane,
Judge of Election, John T. Cox,
Justice Peace, J.W.B. Hegeman,
Com. of Appeals, J. G. Moore,
"   "   Wm. Hughes,
"   "   Rob't Stewart,
Survey'rs Highways, G. H. Miller,
"   "   J. A. Bogart,
Overseer Poor, Ferdinand Ditzel,
Constables, Thomas Gibbins,
"   Albert Kunkel,
Pound Keeper, Wm. C. Wells.

The Appropriations will probably be as follows:—

Support of Poor, $700.
School Purposes, $1800.
Road   " $2000.
Township   " $500.

THE DEATH OF OUR CONTINUED STORY.

We are very sorry to disappoint our boy readers of the thrilling and hair-raising Indian story which has been continued since our first issue; some-one has played us a mean trick and have stolen the copy, which was in book form, containing 375 pages, and entitled: "Young Iron Heart."

Of course we cannot go on with it, and probably it is just as well, as the story was so long, and had we continued it—we never would have lived long enough to finish it.

We don't have to call your attention to our new heading and the general appearance of THE TIMES;—it speaks for itself. We have added to our equipment by purchasing a new press and a quantity of type, etc., so that in the future we will be in better shape to turn out first class job printing and greatly improve the appearance of our miniture publication.

ANOTHER FIRE IN TOWN.

On October 15th, last, at about 11 o'clock P. M., a fire occurred on the premises of Edwin Garthwaite, completely destroying a small cow stable standing in the rear of his barn. It is thought by some, that it was set on fire by tramps. Mr. Garthwaite had no insurance on the building; it was a total loss. Quite a number of "bucket-less spectators" turned out.

Let's start that long-talked-of fire company right now! THE TIMES will head a subscription list with a Five Dollar bill—who'll be the next one?

CRANFORD'S FIRST NEWSPAPER. A national craze for amateur journalism was at its height when sixteen-year-old Emmor K. Adams Jr. edited and published *The Cranford Times* in 1871, the year the township was founded. Adams was a member of the Jersey Blue Amateur Press Association, and he worked out of his Cranford Print Shop and Times Job Office. The paper was only 5 1/8 by 6 1/2 inches in size and was published monthly until its demise in 1872. Among the paper's regular features were a "Jokers Corner" and a list of "uncalled-for letters" to be found at the local post office. This is the Volume II, No. 7, November 1872 edition.

"FAITHFUL AND BELOVED" JUDE. Two women, each described on her tombstone as a "faithful and beloved servant," are buried in the Denman family plot in Fairview Cemetery in Westfield. Jude died in Cranford in 1854 at age forty-two after thirty-nine years with the family. Mary Ann Randolph died in 1880 at age eighty-eight, after sixty years with the Denmans. A manuscript history of the Denman family written in the 1930s refers to both women as slaves. Slavery was a fact of life in antebellum New Jersey, but the law provided that children born to a slave mother after July 4, 1804, would be free, although the mother's owner had the right to their labor until the age of twenty-one for females and twenty-five for males. Had either of these women been a slave, or were they faithful servants?

THE SECOND DENMAN HOMESTEAD IN 1872. This was the second of three Denman houses built on the same foundation. John Denman, the first white settler west of the Rahway in what is now Cranford, built the first house in 1720. This second home was built about 1845 after fire destroyed most of the original house. Located on the 100-acre Denman farm near the corner of Lincoln Avenue and Denman Road, this house was in turn destroyed by fire and replaced by a third home (see p. 66).

STATEMENT

OF

Cash Received & Expended

IN THE

TOWNSHIP OF CRANFORD,

FOR THE YEAR ENDING APRIL 12, 1873.

PRINTED BY ORDER OF THE TOWN COMMITTEE.

Dr.

To balance of Cash on hand from old Committee,.....................	$385.90
To amount of Tax Duplicate,...........15,910.48	
To amount collected of Taxes of 1871,... 83.11	
	$16,379.49

Cr.

By State Tax,.............................	674.00	
" State School Tax,....................1,348.00		
" County Tax........................5,372.69		
" Special School.....................3,600.00		
" Special Road......................800.00		
		11,794.69

Road Accounts.

District No. 1.......................397.29		
" No. 2.........................568.30		
" No. 3.........................430.28		
" No. 4.........................507.11		
		1,902.98

Poor Account.

Paid Eliza Smith for board of Child........108.00	
" Jas. Tierney for rent of rooms 6.00	
" Ira A. Pierson relief of John Wilson.. 10.00	
" Eliza Smith care of Child............. 31.25	
" J. D. Winans for services and Coal... 10.00	
" G. O. Totten groceries in 1871........ 13.77	
" Pat Shay, rent of rooms............. 8.00	
" Dr. McConnell, medicine & attendance 16.05	
" G. E. Ladlow, expenses paid for burying dead horse........................	4.00
" Pat Shay rent of room............. 8.00	
" G. O. Totten, Shoes............. 2.50	
" J. W. B. Hegeman, groceries.........129.00	
" Eliza Smith, care of Child 59.00	
" Isaac Winans, care of tramps....... 14.00	
" Theo. Bluhe, board of C. Kuesen..... 45.00	
" Dr. McConnell, medical attendance... 14.25	
" Eliza Smith, care of Child............108.00	
" Isaac Winans care of tramps & sundries.................	12.25
" Isaac Winans' Salary............... 60.00	
	$659.47

Township Expenses.

Paid I. N. Fisher balance in full for services as Clerk..............	10.50
" W. C. Wells, opening hall............. 7.75	
" Certified copy of Road Law.......... 9.00	
" Stationery.................... 13.00	
" 250 copies of Road Law............. 25.00	
" Int. on Westfield Bond to Mar. 4, 1872 28.14	
" W. C. Wells, care of hall 11.16	
	$104.55

Brought forward,...............104.55	
Paid F. B. Chetwood, legal services..... .. 14.00	
" G. O. Totten, Judge............. .... 10.92	
" W. R. Christmas, services as Clerk...100.00	
" W. C. Wells, opening hall 6.00	
" " preparing hall for Fall election 7.00	
" Interest on Note to Gotleib Nick...... 30.03	
" Interest on Note to J. D. Winans..... 22.24	
" W. R. Christmas, in full for services as Clerk.	125.00
" W. C. Wells 8.00	
" W. D. Bigelow, Judge............. .. 4.00	
" H. J. Phillips " 4.00	
" J. W. Benedict, expenses to Trenton on Cow Disease............	10.60
" Mr. S. B, Mendall, rent of Pound,...... 25.00	
" 500 Blank Road Returns,...............18.00	
" Book for Road Board................. 7.50	
" Notices of Assessments................. 3.50	
" 500 Envelopes,............................. 2.00	
" Filing Road returns,...................10.00	
" Copies of Road returns, and Certificate of County Clerk,...........	11.00
" Postage Stamps, Ink, Paper, &c.......4.50	
" Amount deducted from Tax Duplicate, 43.12	
" Interest paid on Note Discounted in Bank,.............	85.39
" E. K. Adams, Assessor,....... ....150.00	
" S. J. Cox, Road Commissioner,........63.00	
" B. F. Ham, " 63.00	
" J. K. Mills, " 63.00	
" J. A. Elmendorf, " 63.00	
" G. D. Hammar, " 63.00	
" G. O. Totten, Justice,....... ....8.99	
" Moses T. Crane, Salary as Collecter,...200.00	
" M. T. Crane, fees on warrants and payment of School Monies.......	47.29
" For printing tax bills, postage stamps Commissioner of Appeals &c........	27.85
" A. P. Purvis, Town Committee,........40.00	
" G. E. Ladlow " 38.00	
" F. A. Ellis, " 32.00	
" E. S. Crane, " 36.00	
" John Kline, " 32.00	
	$1,583.48
Balance of Cash on hand,.................31.19	
Uncollected Taxes,.................... 407.68	
	$16,379.49

Special Road Tax.

Amount of Assessments..................9652.17		
Amount Collected,....................5,844.86		
" to be " 3,807.31	9,652.17

The sum of $5,844.86 is in Bank on Special Deposit.

Dated CRANFORD, April 12, 1873.

I hereby certify that the above is a true copy of receipts and expenditures, as taken from the books of the Township

WM. R. CHRISTMAS, Town Clerk.

CRANFORD'S MUNICIPAL BUDGET, 1872/73. The township's financial statement for the year ending April 12, 1873, revealed some expenditures not seen today. The "Poor Account" included $4 for burying a dead horse and $14 for the care of tramps. Other monies included $10.60 paid to J.W. Benedict for "expenses to Trenton on Cow Disease" and $25 for rent of the local dog pound. The compiler of these figures, town clerk William R. Christmas, received an annual salary of $125.

A QUESTION OF PRIORITIES, 1875. This cartoon appeared in the August 1, 1875, edition of *The Westfield Townsman*, chiding Cranford for a fire in the "Central House" hotel, where the owner was concerned only with hauling his liquor to safety. Cranford had no fire department, and Westfield's hand-pulled engine came to the rescue. Westfield Fire Foreman Clark delivered "a short, pithy oration" to prevail "upon the youth of Cranford to vacate their roosting place on a rail fence nearby, and assist the department to pass water."

CRANFORD'S ORIGINAL METHODIST CHURCH IN THE EARLY 1870s. The first chapel of the Craneville Methodist Episcopal Church was erected at a cost of $3,500 on Westfield (now Lincoln) Avenue. It was dedicated on May 20, 1863, and the Westfield pastor, the Rev. R.B. Collins, preached every Sunday afternoon. Note the carriage sheds behind the chapel.

THE SECOND FIRST PRESBYTERIAN CHURCH IN 1876. Built in 1869 at a cost of $13,000, this was the second church raised by local Presbyterians since 1851. It was located on the corner of North Union and Springfield Avenues on land purchased from John Grant Crane. It was demolished in 1893, making way for the Romanesque style church on the site today. The area around the church is remarkably open in this view because the town was building on cleared lands of former farms. Note the boardwalks and oil-fed street lamps.

CRANFORD ARISTOCRACY, 1877. The trustees of the Presbyterian Church were among the most influential members of the community, constituting a kind of small-town aristocracy. The trustees were, from left to right, as follows: (seated) William D. Bigelow, Job Williams, John Close, and Emmor K. Adams Sr.; (standing) George Osborn, Frank Ellis, and Josiah Crane Jr. Crane had been a member of the original committee that secured passage of the bill creating the township in 1871.

H.M.S. PINAFORE DOCKED IN CRANFORD, 1880. The Linden Players came to Cranford Hall (at Eastman Street and North Avenue West) to perform what had already become a Gilbert and Sullivan classic. Note the painted backdrop and the kerosene footlights. Cranford Hall also served as the township offices at this time.

FROM PLAYHOUSE TO DOGHOUSE, *c.* 1882. This ornate Victorian playhouse was situated in the gardens of the Alden Bigelow estate at 111 Union Avenue (the site of Cleveland Plaza today). The playhouse was later moved to 24 Eastman Street to serve as an office for William Bigelow Drysdale. Then it was added on to the rear of the house to serve as a room for Mary Jane Drysdale's Great Dane "Derek."

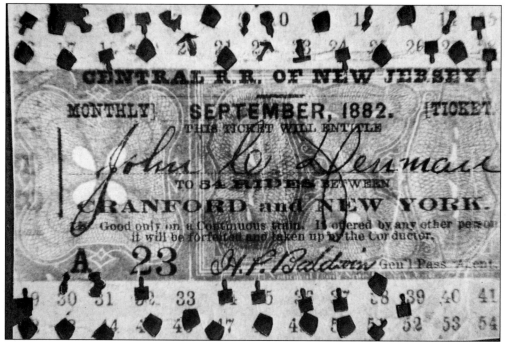

COMMUTER TICKET, 1882. John C. Denman's September 1882 ticket on the Central Railroad of New Jersey was good for fifty-four rides between Cranford and New York, and Denman seems to have missed only five of them. By 1885, Cranford sent seventy-six daily commuters to New York.

JOHN ISENMANN, BUILDER OF BRIDGES. Isenmann (d. 1905) lived on the south side of Springfield Avenue between the river and Central Avenue. A Union County freeholder for twelve years, he was responsible in the 1880s for erecting most of the bridges in Cranford. A fellow freeholder from Summit once asked him how many more bridges in Cranford he would need before he was finished. Isenmann responded that he would not be finished "until I have a large bridge built in the air so I can go up and look down on the other bridges."

THE DAVIS HOME, ABOUT 1885. This farmhouse stood near what is today the northeast corner of Manor Avenue (Willow Avenue in the late nineteenth and early twentieth centuries) and North Union Avenue. The house was nearly a century old when this picture was taken. Union Avenue, just a country lane at that time, did not go beyond this point, and in fact it made a snaking turn to the northwest, as can be seen here.

JOHN HOWARD CROMWELL HOUSE, BUILT IN 1886. John Cromwell moved to Cranford in 1871 and later served as a township commissioner. His home, built in 1886 on Walnut Avenue, is seen here as it looked in the 1950s when it housed an antiques shop. Today the site is occupied by Temple Beth-El.

Arrests.

1887

June 16 John Doe — Swede
          Disorderly conduct   (Tafelski)
Insane   10 days — C.J. — E.K.A. Jr.
                              Sent to morristown

July 25 George Smith — Colored — Light
          Assault & Battery — (Riry
Held for trial — 60 days — C.J.   Case)

Sep. 22 Bridget Robinson — Montd
          Disorderly conduct   } Age 55
D.T.   Discharged — Sent to Newark

Nov. 18 Rebecca Haines — Colored —
          Pettit Larceny
          Age 18 — Short — medium comp.
              Discharged —   E.N. Robbins

1888.
Jan. 25 John Smith (Irish)
          Disorderly & Drunk — Elizabethport
          Age 39 — Dark hair & moustache — 5-8in —
          Geo. G Ely — Comp. — 30 days — C.J. — E.K

1889
Jany 15. John Feminella
          — Bigamy —
              — Italian —   E.K.A.

          leelia Bindenburger — Comp. — C.J.

Feby 3d   Charles Smith — alias Charles
          Jones — Burglary — Age 26   E.K.A.
          Recovered $72.00 Stolen from George G. Ely —

POLICE BLOTTER, 1887-1889. The township's amateur police force, a forty-man organization of "vigilants" incorporated as the Cranford Thief Detecting Society (1869-1889), kept an arrest record. The name of the perpetrator, date of arrest, nationality or race, charge, and disposition of the case were entered. The arresting officer's initials or name were also indicated. The CTDS rarely arrested anyone. In the decade from 1879 to 1889 they made only thirty-five arrests.

18

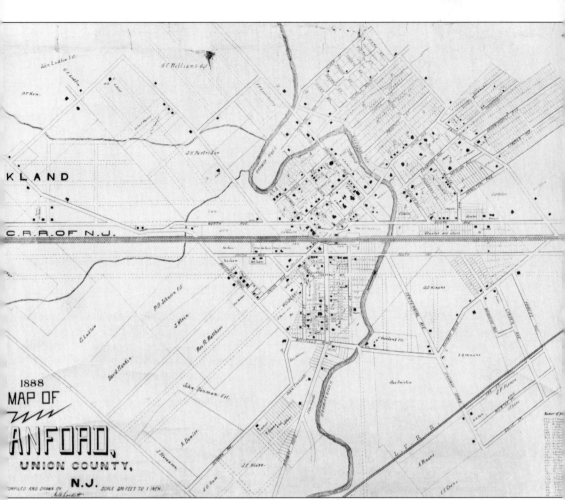

CRANFORD IN 1888. Compiled and drawn by A.M. Lockett, this map of the seventeen-year-old township located existing houses and outbuildings at the time. The village is clustered in the center of the township, close to the river and railroad. Open farm plots surround the center, except in the northeast portion of the township that was already extensively subdivided into lots, although few were occupied. The Oakland section, later Garwood, is undeveloped except for a few buildings near the tracks. A forked-tail mill pond can be seen, branching off the river near Springfield Avenue. Names on many of the plots represent the leading families of the time, founders of the township: Cahill, Ham, Ludlow, Miller, Lounsberry, Winans, Denman, Rankin, and Bigelow. The *New York Star* described Cranford in 1888 as "perhaps the most fashionable New Jersey summer resort for New York society people."

"YGGDRASILL," *c.* 1888. This beautiful home was built in the 1880s for Mrs. Mary Ritchie Bennett at the corner of what is now Prospect Avenue and Riverside Drive, facing the river. She called her home "Yggdrasill," a name drawn from Norse mythology. This was the first home in Cranford to have an elevator. After Mrs. Bennett's death in 1904, the property was operated as the Riverside boardinghouse by Mrs. Fannie Bates.

CRANFORD STALWARTS ROUGHING IT, AUGUST 1888. William Buckley (center, gray suit) and his Cranford companions brought tents, a cook, and a steward to Camp Wa-Wa-Yanda (Wawayanda State Park today) to civilize their sojourn in the woods. The overdressed happy campers sported bicycle caps, tam-o'-shanters, and even a pith helmet. Obviously, bold stripes were quite the thing, and it is hard to separate the jackets from the tents.

CRANFORD RIVER IMPROVEMENT ASSOCIATION REGATTA, 1888. Boaters gathered on the Rahway for the day's aquatic festivities at Bookhout's dock, just upstream from the dam near the North Union Avenue bridge. This is a view of the south bank of the river at the original colonial site of Crane's saw mill.

"SEW-UP TIME" IN THE CHAMBERLAIN HOME, 1889. The harsh glare of a "flash light" is evident in this experimental automatic picture. The boys are doing their lessons in the after-dinner "sew-up time." Five of the six people in the picture are looking at the flash (off to the left) and not at the camera. Note the boys' reflection in the shiny oilcloth table cover. The Chamberlains lived at the corner of North Avenue and Arlington Road.

THERE WAS ALSO IRONING, *c.* 1889. The back porch of this house served as a laundry area, complete with heavy wooden wash tubs, wooden buckets, washboards, and a wicker laundry basket. Water, of course, was drawn from a well and heated on a fire out-of-doors or indoors on a cook stove. Washers and dryers were not yet dreamed of. The house stood on the corner of Elizabeth and Cranford Avenues.

A CRANFORD COWBOY, *c.* 1889. In the late nineteenth century, many Cranford families, while not farmers, kept chickens and perhaps a cow or two. The colonial-era house in the background is the same home shown in the previous picture. Although still open country, this area of the township had been divided (on paper) into building lots by 1889.

A BRIDGE OVER PLACID WATERS, LATE SPRING, 1889. A reminder to "Walk Your Horses" was stenciled on the iron bow of the second Springfield Avenue, or Beadle's, bridge. When a horse and carriage passed over the plank flooring of the bridge, the noise could be heard all over the neighborhood. The Beadle home on the northeast side of Springfield Avenue is in the distance. Note the patch-eyed dog who looks like an old *Our Gang* canine.

WADING ON SPRINGFIELD AVENUE, JULY 1889. It was skirts and trousers up for those who had to contend with the swollen Rahway. In the flood of '89 the water rose 8 feet above normal, covering bridges and cutting off communication between the two sides of the village. These hardy hikers have just come over Beadle's bridge on Springfield Avenue. Note that a portion of the iron fence running from the Beadle home to the bridge (off to the right) has been swept away (see photograph above).

THE P.W. HALL HOUSE IN 1889. Located at 229 Orchard Street, this Bracketed style house, with its carriage house and outbuildings, was typical of the homes built in Cranford for expatriate New Yorkers and Brooklynites during and just after the Civil War. The house was built in 1868 by Nat G. Foster.

SLEDDING ON THE RIVER, c. 1889. A chair sled and a walking sled can be seen in this view of the river in winter. The picture was taken upstream from the Crane's Ford site (off to the left), looking south toward the second Springfield Avenue bridge, then known as Beadle's Bridge.

Two

Casinos, Canoes, and Country Living

1890-1899

THE WALNUT AVENUE BALL CLUB, c. 1890. The Walnut Avenue nine posed with their manager (center, in suit) before a big game. Close inspection of the photograph reveals that the players wore unusual double-buckle baseball belts at that time. That's Alvin Denman sitting on the right.

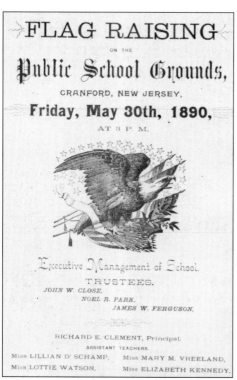

DECORATION DAY FLAG RAISING PROGRAM, MAY 30, 1890. Cranford's school children subscribed to a fund to purchase the flag that was raised at Grant School. The program included recitations, declamations, orations, and an address. Among the "National Airs" sung were "Yankee Doodle," "The Prisoner's Hope," "Marching Though Georgia," and "God Save Our Fatherland."

THE PURVES-MUNOZ HOUSE, ABOUT 1890. Victorian serenity is evident in this photograph of one of Cranford's first great houses. Built in 1864 by Charles Bigelow, it was soon sold to Alexander Purves (Mayor, 1872 to 1875, 1880). Located near the northeast corner of Alden Street and North Union Avenue, the house became the home of the Munoz family in 1880. In the presidential campaign of 1912, President Taft and former President Teddy Roosevelt spoke from the front porch on successive days. The house was razed the following year.

26

SCANDAL IN CRANFORD, 1890. This handbill advertised an article in the July 31, 1890, edition of the *National Police Gazette*. Kittie Bookhout, adopted daughter of a prominent Cranford family, scandalized the community by her long absences from home and by displaying jewelry given to her by a New York lawyer. She was also the sole legatee and "alleged bereaved affianced" of a well-known elderly gentleman in Cranford. Abandoned by her friends, she attempted suicide by taking laudanum. Kittie finally fled Cranford for Long Branch. The *Police Gazette* carried lurid stories of crime, sports reporting, and pictures of girls in tights. Unacceptable for family reading, it was found mainly in saloons and barbershops.

THE NATIONAL

Police Gazette

THE LEADING ILLUSTRATED SPORTING JOURNAL IN AMERICA.

RICHARD K. FOX, Editor and Proprietor, Franklin Square, New York.

Be careful that RICHARD K. FOX'S name as publisher appears on the publication that you purchase from your News Dealer. Respectfully,
RICHARD K. FOX.

NO. 674,

Out Thursday, JULY 31

ILLUSTRATION,

Kittie Bookhout's

ESCAPADES AND HER NUMEROUS FLIRTATIONS CAUSE A SCANDAL AT CRANFORD, N. J.

The POLICE GAZETTE, each week, will illustrate and give all the latest details in relation to the great fight between Joe McAuliffe and Frank P. Slavin, for the POLICE GAZETTE Champion Belt, at London.

THE "BIG SWIMMIN' HOLE," *c.* 1891. Youngsters dove into the Rahway from the riverbank of the "Big Swimmin' Hole," bordering the old Garthwaite farm upstream from Crane's Ford. Another favorite spot was the "Bootjack Swimmin' Hole," at the tip of "The Peninsula" (MacConnell Park today) across the river from Holly Street. The river makes a U-turn there, in the shape of an old-fashioned boot jack.

KNIGHTS OF THE PADDLE, c. 1891. These dashing and eligible boatmen posed with their double paddles and a scull named *Cupid*. The river and canoes once served the "sparking and wooing" purposes that later lovers' lanes and automobiles provided.

A MAN AND HIS POTTED PLANT, c. 1892. Jasper C. Hunt (1844-1917) posed with his rubber plant on the front lawn of "Aldworth," his home at 205 North Union Avenue. Hunt served in 1891 as Cranford's first Democratic mayor. In 1896 he was elected again, this time as a candidate of the reform Citizen's Party. GOP leaders, unable to comprehend how someone other than a Republican could be elected, hired Pinkerton's National Detective Agency to investigate the election. An undercover agent found no evidence of skulduggery.

THE "NEVER PLAYS," AUGUST 27, 1892. This scrub baseball team, composed of nine of the town's more prominent men, had their picture taken just before their game with the "Never Sweats." Players, left to right, were as follows: (seated) E.W. Hadden, James Hibson, Farish Saphar, Edward Hale, and George Teller; (standing) "Commodore" Charles Leo Abry, Emmor K. Adams Jr., Kenyon Messick, and George Littell. The game ended in a 9-9 tie. In the background is the first of Cranford's two casinos under construction.

THE FIRST CASINO, 1892. The first casino building (Cranford Country Club) was designed by Frank T. Lent and built in 1892. A center for social and recreational activities, the club boasted that it was strong in bowling, bicycling, tennis, and dramatics. In January 1897 the building was destroyed by a spectacular fire. That fall, a second casino was erected on the same site.

A WOMAN'S BEST FRIEND, c. 1892. Well-to-do Cranfordians participated in a national craze for big dogs in the 1890s. Here, Florence Bradley is seen with her St. Bernard. By the turn of the century, Miss Bradley was one of New Jersey's top tennis players.

PROFESSOR CORNELIUS A. LEVERIDGE, 1892. Born in New York City, Leveridge moved to Cranford from Westfield in 1869. He financed the move partly through the sale of his extensive collection of geological, historical, and numismatic specimens to P.T. Barnum for display in Barnum's new museum in New York City. In 1882 Leveridge wrote the first history of Cranford. His association with Barnum may account for a couple of the dubious stories he promulgated about Cranford's past, stories that have been repeated for more than one hundred years.

A Midsummer Night's Dream.

NINTH ANNUAL CARNIVAL

Saturday Evening, Aug. 11, 1894.

GENERAL ILLUMINATION OF HOUSES, GROUNDS AND BOATS.
TWO PROCESSIONS OF BOATS, AND TWO FULL BANDS.

The Cranford Boating Association cordially invite you to assist them all you can, by making as much light as possible on your boats, also in and around your houses.

All those taking part in the great processions of boats are requested to be ready at half-past seven P. M.

Boats kept near the dam will please join the procession at that part of the river. Those near the upper end will kindly form in line above Hampton Hall.

One band will be stationed at the bend of the river near the Club House, and the other in the grove, between the Eastman Street bridge and the foot bridge.

At eight o'clock a rocket will be discharged as a notice to both processions to start.

The boats will proceed slowly to the opposite end of the course, and return to the starting point, keeping at least twenty-five feet apart, and are requested not to break the lines until orders are given.

GEO. HARVEY MILLER,

D. H. CARDOZO,   *Commodore.*

Secretary.

P. S.—It is earnestly hoped that everything in the shape of a boat or canoe that can float and carry at least a half dozen Chinese lanterns, will take part in the procession.

In case of rain the Carnival will be postponed to Saturday, August 18th, or the next fair Saturday.

A MIDSUMMER NIGHT'S DREAM, 1894. The Cranford Boating Association's Ninth Annual Carnival took place on the Rahway on Saturday evening, August 11, 1894. This handbill advertising the event asked for "everything in the shape of a boat or canoe that can float" to be put on the river. The nighttime river procession began with the firing of a signal rocket.

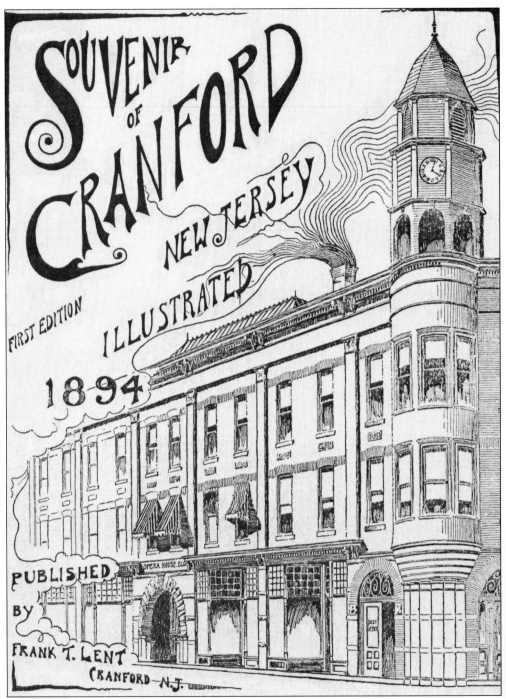

SOUVENIR OF CRANFORD, 1894. Frank T. Lent was a well-known suburban architect and author of *Sound Sense in Suburban Architecture* and *Sensible Suburban Residences*. He designed the Opera House Block (North Avenue from Eastman to North Union), which appeared on the cover of his *First Edition* publication promoting Cranford building sites and homes.

CIVIL WAR VETERAN WILLIAM D. WOOD IN 1894. "Billy" Wood served four annual terms as Cranford's mayor: 1879, 1881, 1883, and 1884. His military background served him well in the 1870s when he was captain of the Cranford Thief Detecting Society.

TENNIS ANYONE? *c.* 1894. Lawn tennis was a popular diversion for Cranford residents, as can be seen by the number of players on the ten well-manicured courts behind the casino. The players' costumes were quite formal; the approach to the game looks rather casual.

FIREMEN'S PARADE, 1895. It was a chilly autumn morning on North Avenue East as the new Gleason & Baily ladder truck belonging to Hook & Ladder Company No. 1 drove past the ten-member Fife & Drum Corps of the rival Cranford Union Hose Company. The narrow stone building behind the truck stands today, wedged between newer structures.

O, THE FOLLY OF DRINK! c. 1896. The bar of the Cranford Hotel, owned by Martin Hess, was generally considered the most elegant drinking establishment in Cranford. Seen here are some booted regulars who have come in for a nickel beer. Note the spittoons and the floor stained with tobacco juice.

THE CRANFORD HIGH SCHOOL
MAGAZINE, 1896. The *Cranford Student*
was first published by CHS students in
January 1896. At that time the three high
school classes were housed with the lower
grades in Public School No. 1, the first of
two successive buildings known as Grant
School. The slick monthly publication
contained school notes, commentary on
world events, fiction, and poetry. One
writer of scientific bent estimated the daily
water consumption of the students at "80
gallons, or more than 30 pailfuls—nearly
three barrels, to be pumped in the cellar
and carried to the several classrooms."

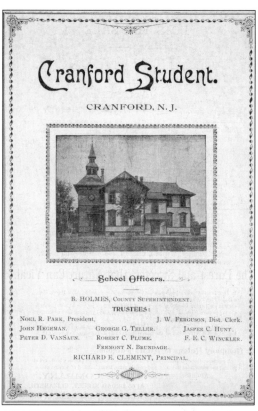

FAIR ACRES DRIVING CLUB, *c.* 1896. New money and increased leisure time led to the
establishment of this club and track for trotters and pacers. Although officially located in
Westfield, the track's northeast turn cut through a portion of Cranford, just off Gallows Hill
Road near Fairview Cemetery.

THE SECOND EDITION OF THE *CRANFORD CITIZEN*. E.R. Clyma's March 12, 1898, issue of this Saturday paper featured a sketch of "The New Holly Street School" (Grant School), for which ground had just been broken. Sharing the front page was an illustration and article on a Kentucky steer with a wooden leg. A page-three ad placed by a jealous Westfield realtor favored that town over Cranford because Westfield "has no creek wandering thro' the town to breed malaria and mosquitoes."

THE POTTER-CHRONICLE BUILDING, *c.* 1899. Also known as Assembly Hall or Cranford's Flat-Iron Building, this building at North and North Union Avenues (both unpaved) was erected in 1897 by John A. Potter to house the offices of the *Cranford Chronicle*. On the left, at the edge of the sidewalk, is a sign for Charley Sing's Laundry and another sign saying "Rail Road Crossing Look Out For The Locomotive." Unfortunately, many people did not heed the warning. The building was torn down in 1926 when the state widened North Avenue. Today the site is Eastman Plaza.

THE FIRST SPERRY HOME, ABOUT 1899. Madame's carriage awaits in this view of Thomas A. Sperry's first Cranford home. Built for S & H Green Stamp Company founder Sperry in 1898, the house was later sold to Charles Hansel, who lived in it until he built his house on Springfield Avenue (Grey Funeral Home today). Located at 319 North Union Avenue, this first Sperry house stands in magnificent condition today.

AN ELEGANT MODE OF TRAVEL, c. 1899. In the days before automobiles, when gentlemen prided themselves on fine carriage horses, Thomas Sperry always had the finest horses and the best driver. Outside the stable at 319 North Union Avenue, Fred Williams, Sperry's coachman, wearing a high silk hat and with whip in hand, had his spirited team ready for a drive.

Three
The Venice of New Jersey
1900-1909

THE 7:47 PULLING IN, 1900. Commuters walked out on the tracks to hop aboard a morning train to New York. The station and tracks were at grade level at that time. As early as 1890 it was noted that forty-four trains stopped daily at Cranford.

A STAIRWAY CHAT, OCTOBER 1900. The women of the Merriam family paused to have this picture taken in the entrance hall of their Union Avenue home. Note the stuffed alligator (or is it a cayman?) on the floor holding a tray for receiving calling cards. What does his grinning welcome say about this household?

THE PARROTTS COME TO CRANFORD, ABOUT 1900.

New Yorkers were not the only ones to move to Cranford. Between 1885 and 1905 the African-American population of Cranford increased from 46 to 279, with most of the increase the result of newcomers arriving from the South, particularly Virginia. Some came from farther away, however. Pictured here are Walter Charles Parrott (left) and his wife Laura Jones Parrott, who left Sparta, Georgia, for Cranford about 1900. Walter's brother William (right) did not come north.

CRANFORD DEPOT, ABOUT 1901. A train is pulling out in this view looking east from the junction of North Union Avenue and North Avenue (on the left). The station, built in 1865, is in the distance in the center of the picture. Cranford had about four hundred daily commuters to New York at this time, each paying $6.30 a month.

HORSE-DRAWN DELIVERY, *c.* 1902. Driver Harry Pederson held the reins of the brand-new delivery rig belonging to the H.G. Bowers store. Owner Harry G. Bowers, who was assistant president of the Union Hose No. 1 fire company, sold hay, grain, feed, and horse and stable equipment from his store at "1 Bank Building."

THE CRANFORD BASEBALL CLUB, 1902. Team members struck a collectively self-confident pose in an era when striped shirts and striped socks were in fashion. The members kneeling were, from left, Ray Cox, Harry Vorhees, Bert Hibson, and Jake Derby; standing were unknown, Bill Plummer, Jim McMahon, "Henry" Moore, Wilbur Tusch, unknown, and Bill Johnson. The youngster in front (unidentified) was the mascot, without whom it seems no team could function. Note the overstuffed catcher's mitt he is holding.

PLOWING THROUGH, c. 1902.
Central Railroad of New Jersey engine
No. 60 plowed a path through deep
snow near the Walnut-Union grade
crossing in downtown Cranford. The
Potter-Chronicle Building can be seen
in the background, the site of Eastman
Plaza today.

LEHMAN'S GROCERY, 1903. The
opening of this elegant grocery store
was a big event in Cranford. Located in
the Masonic Building on the corner of
Alden Street and North Union
Avenue, Lehman's employed eight
persons, either in the store or on
delivery wagons, and as the *Chronicle*
said, the goods were "in every way first
class." There were even chairs for
weary shoppers. On the back wall the
shelves were lined with bottles of wine
and liquor "for medicinal use."

MRS. HOOVER'S PRIVATE SCHOOL, 1904. Since 1897 Mrs. A.J. Hoover had conducted a private school in this house. With her "corps of teachers," Mrs. Hoover taught primary and kindergarten pupils of both sexes. The house is still there, at 113 Miln Street, home to a media company.

A NEW STUDEBAKER, 1904. Adelaide Bigelow Drysdale posed with her equine and canine friends in her new Studebaker buckboard. The scene is at the carriage sheds that were behind 24 Eastman Street.

GARWOOD PROMOTION, 1904. In 1903 the rapidly industrializing district on the west side of Cranford broke away from the township to incorporate as the Borough of Garwood. Once known as Oakland, the area had a separate identity and was called Garwood as early as 1894. This ad appeared in a 1904 promotional book, *Cranford Illustrated*. The tiny, one-year-old municipality of Garwood was touted as "a wide-awake town for wide-awake people," and the ad mentions that eight factories were already in operation.

ST. MICHAEL'S CHURCH, ABOUT 1905. This was the second Church of St. Michael, the Archangel. It was built in 1901 at the corner of Miln and Alden Streets, after a fire destroyed the first church on the corner of Elizabeth and Bloomingdale Avenues. In 1909 this second church was raised above ground level in order to include a basement auditorium, making it higher than what we see in this picture. The frame and shingle church was demolished in 1949 to make way for the Romanesque brick structure of today.

THE ICE BOY COMETH, c. 1905. Clarence Schmitz (center) and the two older boys worked for M.F. Wheeler's Cranford Ice Company on South Avenue. Ice was packed in straw to keep it from melting, and it was delivered for use in charcoal-lined ice boxes in the kitchens of Cranford homes. In 1905 a human body was found in Echo Lake, where Wheeler cut his ice. It had been there all winter. After that, Wheeler got his ice supply for household use from a manufacturer who used distilled water.

THE PAUSE THAT REFRESHES, c. 1905. On a Sunday afternoon river outing, a parade of canoes filled with women and girls in white summer frocks paused for a drink at a bubbling spring along the Rahway in Cranford. The location of this spring is lost to us today. Would we drink from it if we found it?

THE BENNETT DOCK, c. 1905. With a massive weeping willow as a backdrop, this boat pavilion on the Rahway was part of the Mary R. Bennett estate (see p. 20). It was situated on the north bank of the river at the junction of Riverside Drive and Prospect Avenue. The view looks downstream, or southeast, toward the North Union Avenue bridge hidden in the trees in the distance.

THE "LILY OR THE ROSE," JULY 15, 1905. A prize-winning entry in the boat parade of the 1905 Cranford River Carnival was this floral canoe. The float's title probably refers to the frequent juxtaposition of the lily and rose in poetry and the question of which flower was most fair. The scene was the Moore property across from the Porcella boathouse at 207 Holly Street.

PURE FOOD CRUSADER ALICE LAKEY. A one-time president of the Cranford Village Improvement Association, stern-visaged Alice Lakey (1857-1935) gained fame as a reformer and national leader in the Pure Food Movement. Her greatest achievement was in mobilizing support for the Pure Food and Drug Act of 1906. Working through women's clubs, she directed a petition campaign that was instrumental in persuading the U.S. Senate to pass the act. Under Lakey's leadership, women influenced the passage of federal legislation fourteen years before they gained the right to vote.

PAVING SPRINGFIELD AVENUE, c. 1907. This steam-belching contraption poured out concrete for the first paving of a portion of Springfield Avenue. At the time, the avenue was just a single-lane dirt road. The scene was photographed in front of the John Pierson property.

LAZY, HAZY DAYS OF SUMMER, c. 1907. No fiberglass poles, nylon lines, or spinning reels here. A line, crude hook, and a pole made from a tree branch sufficed for these young followers of Isaak Walton, angling in the Nomahegan area. Cranford's "crooked river" afforded escape, serenity, and sport to young and old alike in years gone by.

BUILDING THE SKEETER CLUB, WINTER 1908. A dozen young men salvaged lumber and tar paper to build a clubhouse on the banks of the Rahway. Several board fences came up missing that winter. Located behind Central Avenue, southwest of Springfield Avenue, the Skeeter Club was one of several canoe clubs that existed along the river at various times.

CENTRAL RAILROAD OF NEW JERSEY BRIDGE, 1908. This massive old stone bridge with its triple arches spanned the Rahway just a few blocks east of the central downtown area. Note the fashionably dressed young lady leaning against the tree on the riverbank on the right. The site where she is standing had been the location of river baptisms for the First Baptist Church until the late 1890s

CRANFORD STATION, ABOUT 1909. Built in 1906 at a cost of $45,000, this Cranford railroad station replaced an earlier one in use since 1865 (see p. 41). The new station, which even had a brick fireplace inside, was considered the finest on the line between Scranton, Pennsylvania, and Jersey City, New Jersey. The station was demolished when the process of track elevation began in 1928.

STATION PLAZA, 1909. It was a foggy winter day when this photograph of Cranford's twin station buildings was taken. The view looks southwest from atop a building on North Avenue East. Chickens roamed the grassy plot in the foreground.

ARBOR DAY AT GRANT SCHOOL, MAY 1909. Decked out in their Sunday best, these youngsters participated in the planting of a large sapling in the front lawn of Grant School. Located on the corner of Holly Street and Springfield Avenue, this second Grant School was built in 1898 and razed in 1975.

LABOR DAY RACES, 1909. A flag-draped finish line was stretched across the Rahway just downstream from the first Springfield Avenue (Isenmann) bridge, awaiting the day's canoe races. This was the annual New Jersey Canoe Association Regatta, usually held in Cranford.

Four
Lemonade Socials and War
1910–1919

A FALSE ALARM IN 1910. E.K. Adams Jr. took this picture of the Cranford Fire Department's hose carriage (left) and ladder truck (right) as four chargers pulled them out onto North Avenue, heading west. The call proved to be a false alarm. In the background is the brick firehouse, dedicated just the year before.

FALLS ON THE RAHWAY AT DROESCHER'S MILL, c. 1910. Severin Droescher installed floodgates on the dam and constructed fieldstone retaining walls along the banks of the river as part of his Lincoln Park development. The work included a footbridge, river overlook, and stone gazebo. The walled center island (extreme right in picture) is gone today, and Droescher's efforts lie in ruins.

SEVERIN R. DROESCHER. A native of Germany, Severin Droescher (1867-1936) emigrated to the United States in 1881. He came to Cranford in 1901 and bought the historic Williams-Vreeland Mill, where he manufactured razor hones and barber supplies. Investing heavily in real estate, he developed the area of Lincoln Park. Always active in civic affairs, Droescher served on the Board of Chosen Freeholders in the middle 1920s.

THE DROESCHER RESIDENCE IN 1911. Built *c.* 1820, this country home, with its summer awnings and wellhouse, once stood adjacent to Droescher's Mill, then known as the Cranford Oil Stone Works. The mill and house were owned by Severin Droescher. Notice that the curbs and sidewalk were new in this picture, but Lincoln Avenue was still unpaved. Until it was torn down in 1937, the house was located near the corner of Lincoln Avenue and today's Lincoln Park East.

'POSSUM WITH THE FIXIN'S, YUMMY! 1911. When the Cranford Canoe Club held its fourth annual dinner on February 4, 1911, the menu featured something different— opossum. Tradition has it that the members turned up their noses at the delicacy. The *Cranford Citizen*, however, reported that "after the possum with all the good fixin's had been put away, smoking was indulged in and speeches were in order." The paper added that the "members lingered at the festive board until after midnight."

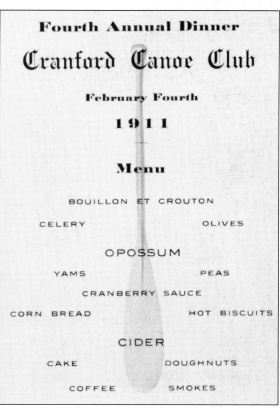

Fourth Annual Dinner

Cranford Canoe Club

February Fourth

1911

Menu

BOUILLON ET CROUTON

CELERY   OLIVES

OPOSSUM

YAMS   PEAS

CRANBERRY SAUCE

CORN BREAD   HOT BISCUITS

CIDER

CAKE   DOUGHNUTS

COFFEE   SMOKES

FIRE HORSE TRIALS, c. 1912. Local breeders, farms, and stables supplied horses for try-outs to become Cranford Fire Department "chargers." In the photograph above, a beauty stood in front of the bay doors of the firehouse on North Avenue East. In the bottom photograph a fine matched pair easily pulled the hook and ladder truck through the mud of Springfield Avenue.

"RAHWAY RIVER, CRANFORD, N.J. ROYAL BLUE LINE," c. 1912. The Baltimore & Ohio Railroad–Central Railroad of New Jersey published a series of postcards promoting scenic vacation areas along the route served by the Royal Blue Line Dining Car Service. The Rahway River in Cranford was one of the attractions.

ICE CREAM DREAMS, c. 1912. Customers could purchase this postcard of the interior of "Our Drug Store" in downtown Cranford. J.R. Reay's Cranford Pharmacy, opened in 1904 at 15 Union Avenue, was famous for its magnificent marble soda fountain, seen on the left.

NORTH UNION AVENUE BRIDGE, ABOUT 1912. Looking north across the bridge we can see the Ellis mansion on the right, located on the south corner of Forest and North Union Avenues. Built about 1868, the house was remodeled in 1898, giving it the look of a great Southern plantation house. Thomas A. Sperry owned the house in the early 1900s and called it "Linwold."

ADVERTISING CRANFORD, 1912. These ads are from a program for a "Grand Minstrel Show" presented in the Cranford Opera House by the Degree Team, Cranford Court of the Independent Order of Foresters, on January 12, 1912. Henry Dreyer's Sunny Crest Produce Farm on Springfield Avenue is still in business (now Dreyer's Farms), but John Schindler's horse-shoeing and blacksmith shop on Union Avenue is long since gone.

Life in Cranford

the VENICE of New Jersey

"LIFE IN CRANFORD," 1913. S & H Green Stamp magnate William Miller Sperry (1858-1927) also dabbled in local real estate, as can be seen by this 1913 advertisement. Among the township's listed attractions were the "Lowest Death Rate and Best Water in the State." You, too, could move to Cranford and have your own pony.

THE DREAM TEAM, 1913. They wore tennis shoes, but one has to wonder just how fast these young ladies could get around the court in those ankle-length skirts. Two of the players wore baggy bloomers tucked into their socks. It is interesting to note that the game of basketball was only twenty-two years old at the time this picture was taken. James Naismith started it all in Springfield, Massachusetts, in 1891 using two peach baskets and a soccer ball.

THE FIREBOAT *GEORGE C. MOON*, 1913. Named in honor of Cranford's fire commissioner, this canoe-based float won first prize in the novelty class in the 1913 River Carnival. Built by members of the Cranford Fire Department, the model fire boat was patterned on those used in New York Harbor.

THE 1914 RIVER CARNIVAL. Ready for the start of the carnival, these heavily decorated floats waited in front of the Cranford Canoe Club (later the Girl Scout House). We can see the USS *Texas*, the battleship *New Jersey*, a Venetian gondola, the ferryboat *Cranford*, and a Japanese-lantern bedecked canoe on the right, which seems to be piloted by four ninjas (in the U.S. in 1914?).

TROLLEY TRESTLE, ABOUT 1914. For many years trolley riders to and from Elizabeth crossed over the B & O Railroad tracks on the trestle shown here. It was a familiar and unsightly landmark on Cranford's eastern border. Built in 1900, shortly after the trolley line was completed, the trestle began at South Avenue and Lincoln Avenue East, turned southeast, then curved back northeast to South Avenue again. The trestle's concrete piers stood until 1940, several years after trolley service had ended.

ROYAL ARCANUM FLOAT, c. 1915. Powered by paddlers behind a trellis, this River Carnival entry featured three young ladies representing Virtue, Mercy, and Charity, the motto of this secret, fraternal benefit society. Founded in 1877, the Royal Arcanum promised "Life Insurance at minimum cost" and "Social Features, elevating and instructive." The Cranford Council of the R.A. was instituted in 1892. Nearly all of the prominent men in Cranford were members.

THE ULHIGH CANOE CLUB, 1915. Built in 1908, this familiar building on the corner of Orange and Springfield Avenues was privately operated as a canoe livery for many years. Later known as the Cranford Canoe Club (one of two clubs with that name), the business was purchased by the township in 1990. It is now operated as a concession.

1914 CRANFORD FIRE ALARM 1915

Fire Headquarters Telephone 43   Chief's Telephone, 314-J

LOUIS M. HESS, CHIEF

INSTRUCTIONS.

All public boxes have glass key guards. To give an alarm break the glass, turn the key and open the door, pull down the hook on the inside, and then let go.

Every person should acquaint himself with the nearest box to his residence, so that in case of fire valuable moments may be saved.

No person should give more than one alarm of the same fire without an order from the Chief or his associates.

LOCATION OF BOXES.

Box	Location
17	Corner Walnut and South Avenues.
18	Union Avenue, corner North Avenue.
19	Fire House.
28	Union Avenue and Claremont Place.
37	Lincoln and Centennial Avenues.
46	Lincoln and Union Avenues.
53	North Avenue and Orchard Street.
62	Linden and Orange Avenues.
145	Hampton and Eastman Streets.
217	Arlington Road and North Avenue.
235	Holly Street and Springfield Avenue.
415	Lincoln and Walnut Avenues.

FIRE ALARM CARD, 1914-1915. Cranford Fire Chief Louis M. Hess issued this card listing the locations of all twelve of the township's fire-alarm boxes. The alarms were located principally in the downtown, or central, district. Chief Hess was not averse to adding an advertisement for his plumbing business to the card.

THE ITALIAN MISSION, 1915. In the second year of World War I, this Cranford group was organized through the local Methodist church to aid war-torn Italy. Among those standing beside the Reverend John Hancock Methodist Episcopal Church on Walnut Avenue were F.B. Ham (first on left), Antonio San Giuliano (sixth from left), Nicholas Polidoro (center, under window), young Michael Colaneri (holding picture), and Joseph Iaione (extreme right). Mr. Ham taught Sunday school classes for English-speaking children, and Mr. Polidoro taught the Italian class.

"THE BEST WALKER IN CRANFORD," 1917. Eldridge Humphrey of North Avenue East was a champion pedestrian, famed for his sixty-mile Cranford to Camp Wawayanda jaunts and a hike to Massachusetts. A holder of several records for long-distance walks, Humphrey was a star CHS athlete, Class of '17. Upon graduation from high school during World War I, he enlisted in the Canadian Army but switched to the U.S. Marine Corps when America went "over there." After the war he moved to Pennsylvania, where he became a state trooper.

OVER THE TOP-- AND BEYOND!

The Personal Experiences of Famous Fighters
————RECOUNTED BY THEMSELVES————

BAYONET FIGHTING!

Illustrated by Veterans of the Western Front

Official British Army Pictures
OF

THE BATTLE OF ARRAS!

Described by One of the Combatants While the Picture is Being Shown

SCOTCH PIPERS!   TRENCH MUSIC!

Through the courtesy of the British and Canadian Recruiting Mission

Under the Auspices of the Cranford Home Guard, N. J. S. M. R.

For the Benefit of the New York Sun Tobacco Fund for the

BOYS "OVER THERE"

Cranford Theatre, Thursday, April 25th

8:15 P. M.

ADMISSION, 50c   No Reserved Seats

Tickets on Sale at Reay's and The Apollo

BAYONETS IN THE STREETS OF CRANFORD, APRIL 25, 1917. America was a neophyte in World War I. In order to pump up patriotism, the Cranford Home Guard sponsored a live appearance by several uniformed British soldiers supplied by the British and Canadian Recruiting Mission. In a program at the Cranford Theater (Hartig's Paint Store today) they narrated a silent film on the Battle of Arras (April 9 to May 3, 1917) and played "trench music" on bagpipes. The soldiers also demonstrated bayonet fighting on the street outside the theater.

BANNER DAY AT CLEVELAND SCHOOL, *c.* 1918. This patriotic rally took place during the World War I period in the Cleveland School yard. Note the white-uniformed youngsters. The occasion was the official transfer of the class banner. The homes in the background lined North Union Avenue.

"ELM HAVEN" IN 1918. The third and last of the Denman homesteads replaced an earlier *c.* 1845 house that burned (see p. 11). Located at 4 Denman Road, then a country lane, "Elm Haven" was razed in 1951. The carriage house behind the main building survived and was moved to 3 Burnside Avenue and remodeled as a home.

BORN IN THE CASINO. Edith (left) and Ruth Evans were the daughters of Lemuel and Irene Evans. Lemuel Evans was steward of the Cranford Casino on Riverside Drive. Both girls were born in the casino, Ruth in 1900 and Edith in 1910. Here, the young ladies were photographed in 1918 gathering roses in front of the Sperry-Goodrich greenhouse adjacent to the casino. Ruth became a teacher in Princeton, New Jersey, and Edith became a social worker in New York City.

CHAPLAIN CANNON, 1918. The Rev. David Cannon (1879-1943) was installed as pastor of the First Baptist Church of Cranford in September 1911. He left in November 1918 to become an army chaplain. A graduate of Lincoln University, he received his training at Princeton Theological Seminary. The Rev. Cannon was the father of three scholar-educators, the best known of whom is longtime Cranford resident Dr. Deborah Partridge Wolfe.

A CRANFORD MEMBER OF THE "LOST BATTALION." Lt. Joseph P. Hever was ready for action with his holstered .45 and gas mask bag in this portrait taken in wartime France. As an officer in the 307th Infantry, 77th Division, Hever participated in the Meuse-Argonne offensive where he and several companies and platoons from different units were encircled in a ravine by the Germans. After a heroic defense against great odds, they were finally relieved. Ironically, the "Lost Battalion," famed in film and story, was neither lost nor a battalion.

A "JUDGE OF PROPELLERS." William A. Hale (CHS class of '12) graduated from Stevens Institute in 1916 and joined the army. In 1917 he was assigned as a traveling judge of propellers in the airplane engineering department. His task was to guarantee the safety of the flying machines being sent with aviators to France. On July 5, 1918, just before he went up from Curtis Field (in Buffalo, New York) on what was to be his last flight, he was told that someone else could make the flight for him. The twenty-four-year old Hale responded, "It's my duty." A blood-stained letter found on his body after the crash testified that he had a premonition of his own death.

BRIG. GEN. WADE HAMPTON HAYES, 1919. Seen here in his earlier Lt. Colonel's uniform, Virginia-born Hayes (1879–1956) moved to Cranford upon his marriage in 1905. In World War I he was on the staff of General Pershing, and at the conclusion of the war he became colonel of the famed 7th Regiment in New York City. Although transferred to London in 1928, Gen. Hayes maintained a residence in Cranford until 1939. In World War II, Hayes led a unit of the American Home Guard, a forty-man motorized squadron of American businessmen who served as the bodyguard for the British commander of the London area.

THREE CRANFORD "DEVIL DOGS," JULY 1919. The Germans called U.S. Marines "devil dogs," but these three marines from Cranford preferred to call themselves "The Three Musketeers." In this photograph taken at Brest in France were (left to right) Harold "Pin" Chamberlain, George Schindler, and Elliot Moody. In later years Moody was a longtime trustee of the Cranford Historical Society.

CRANFORD "DOUGHBOYS" IN FRANCE, 1919. Two Cranford servicemen, Marvin D. Hall (left) and Lt. Dean Mathey, met at Cannes, France, a few months after the close of World War I. Mathey later became an internationally ranked tennis star.

HOLT vs. MATHEY, SEPTEMBER 1919. Amateur boxing matches were held as part of Cranford's "Welcome Home" celebration for the men and women of World War I. Bouts were three rounds of three minutes each of "good, clean sport." Mayor John Roach stopped one fight after a contender received a broken jaw.

Five
Cranford Dresses Up
1920-1929

THE CRYSTAL SET, NOVEMBER 1921. Cranford farmer and carpenter Charles J. Fox is seen here in his neighbor's kitchen tuning in an Aeriola Jr. crystal set. The picture was actually an advertising photograph meant to influence farmers to purchase radios. The set retailed for $99.

HOME FROM "OVER THERE," 1920. Cranford's medal-bedecked soldiers, sailors, and marines posed for a commemorative picture in the Cleveland School yard (today's Cleveland Plaza). Sitting, from left to right, are Dan Arnold, Mortimer Gross Jr., an unidentified chaplain from Roselle Park, Ed Cruickshank, and Herb Winckler; kneeling are Mr. MacNamara, John Ryan, Clarence Schmitz, unknown, Bernard Yansch, Charles Lanza, Luco Buonocore, two unknowns, Frank Lenz, Phil Keenan, and unknown; standing (front row) are Harry Craig, Bob Schaffner, Larry Brennan, Ted Chamberlain, Penney Aldrich, Dudley Croft, Ray Tool, two unknowns, John Whitham, Jack Stoltz, George Schindler, unknown, and Russell Freeman; and standing (back row) are unknown, Ed Last, Dick Dowdell, unknown, John Iannaccone, Crescent Iannaccone, Bennie Lee, and Archie LaVar.

CRANFORD BOY SCOUT WILLIAM KLEIN, 1920. A tragic accident in the summer of 1920 set back scouting in Cranford for a period of time. On an official outing at Westerly, Rhode Island, Cranford scouts Bill Klein and Edwin Lewis drowned in heavy surf on July 15, 1920. The entire township of Cranford was in mourning for months thereafter. This photograph of the fifteen-year old Klein was taken on that outing.

CRANFORD THEATRE

Vol. VI.   WEEK OF MARCH 7, 1921   No. 16

Carmel Myers

(Universal Star)

CRANFORD THEATER FLYER, MARCH 7, 1921. Universal Pictures silent-film star Carmel Myers was featured on the front page of this weekly four-page flyer. Among the coming attractions was Sessue Hayakawa in *Li Ting Lang*, a tale of "thrilling conflict between race and love." Comedy shorts, cartoons, serials, and the Pathe News also played with each feature. Unlike today, the feature film was changed daily, although sometimes held over a second day. Evening tickets in 1921 were 25¢ each.

73

EXEMPT FIREMEN'S CELEBRATION, JUNE 2, 1921. A flashing electric "Welcome" sign (above the bunting) greeted all of Cranford's living exempt firemen, many of whom were with the first two fire companies founded in 1892/93. Among those attending were old-timers Gideon Ludlow (front row, center, with whiskers) and CFD founder Emmor K. Adams Jr. (right, in white cap).

AT CRANFORD STATION, JULY 1921. A Cranford police officer directed traffic in front of the tile-roofed Jersey Central Railroad station. The sign in the background promoted Cranford's Golden Jubilee. The township's fifty-year birthday party on July 2, 3, and 4 included a Mardi Gras parade, block dance, river carnival, and school historic pageant.

MINSTREL BAND, 1921. Old-time minstrel shows with their blackface makeup and insulting caricatures were overtly racist. Unfortunately, they were also quite popular and quite common. Here the Young Men's Bible Class of the First Presbyterian Church posed in white uniforms as a blackface band for Cranford's Golden Jubilee on July 2, 1921.

SCOUT TROOP 76 BASKETBALL TEAM, c. 1922. Father Kenneth D. Martin (right) was scoutmaster and coach for this Boy Scout junior team sponsored by St. Michael's Church. In front, left to right, are E. Fay, unknown, Chester Wood, and Clint Fraser; in back are Jud Chapin, Phil Tomlinson, Morris Briscoe, and Ron Witham.

CRANFORD

The Venice of New Jersey

By RAPID TROLLEYS *and* EXCELLENT ❖AUTO❖ ROADS

By THROUGH TRAINS *and* ❖RAPID JITNEYS❖

easy to reach

over 90 TRAINS *daily*

❖excellent automobile roads ❖jitneys❖
fast trolley service *and* station buses

CRANFORD WAS "EASY TO REACH," c. 1922. This is a panel from a poster-size folder promoting real estate in Orchard Park, "a highly restricted residential section" on Cranford's north side. Ease of access to transportation was emphasized. The township was listed as having a population of 6,000 living "only 17 miles from New York." Cranford was served by "over 90 trains daily," rapid trolleys, "excellent auto roads," and rapid jitneys (buses). The promotion agreed that "the State Board of Health told the truth when they referred to Cranford as one of the most healthful and picturesque spots in the entire state." It was further emphasized that "the hard working man who seeks that haven of happiness and comfort for his family and self will find the realization of his fondest dreams in CRANFORD—just a step from city hustle to peaceful country ease."

NORTH AVENUE, FROM ALDEN STREET AND NORTH UNION AVENUE, 1922. Downtown Cranford of almost eighty years ago was not the clean, tidy, and colorful area it is today. He we see shops along North Avenue East, including M. Aamodt Furniture and the American Lunch. Dual smokestacks rising in the distance included one for the Public Service trolley power house on South Avenue.

NORTH AVENUE AT SPRINGFIELD AVENUE, 1922. Looking west along North Avenue, one can see that homes still lined the south side of the recently macadamized street. Burke's Garage (right) pumped gas and was the town's authorized Dodge dealer. In the 1920s most new cars in small towns and rural areas were sold by garages and service stations rather than by showrooms.

INTERSECTION OF NORTH AVENUE WEST AND MILN STREET, OCTOBER 21, 1922. Trees predominate in this downtown view. The familiar township flag mast can be seen in the plaza on the left. Nathan's Variety Store, Plaza Soda and Cigars, the Mutual G-Way Company grocery, and Reze Shoes are some of the shops that can be glimpsed in the distance along Eastman Street. An empty lot and a gasoline pump from the Standard station can be seen on the right, where the Cranford Theater is today. The road was unpaved. To the right center of the picture is the Chronicle Building, site of Eastman Plaza today.

WRECK AT THE GRADE CROSSING, 1924. On the morning of August 21, 1924, a Philadelphia and Reading commuter train crashed into a heavy truck at the Lincoln Avenue grade crossing, killing four men and injuring many others. Here, curious onlookers surveyed the damage. This accident brought the number of fatalities at the Union and Lincoln Avenue grade crossings to seven since the beginning of 1923. The *Cranford Citizen and Chronicle* denounced the grade crossings as "death traps."

CRANFORD HORSE SHOW PROGRAM, 1924. Begun in 1923 and sponsored by the Cranford Riding Club, the Cranford Horse Show ran annually well into the 1930s. The show averaged two hundred entries and four thousand spectators a year, making it a major event for New Jersey's elite equestrians. The show was held at the Kensington Riding School on the Boulevard in Kenilworth. The school advertised thirty miles of "country and woodland bridle paths" in adjacent Union County parks. Proceeds from the horse show were divided among Cranford charities. In 1932 local equestrians starred in a movie, *The Romance of Cranford*, filmed at the Kensington school.

SECOND ANNUAL

Cranford Horse Show
Cranford Riding Club
Saturday, Oct. 4, 1924
Kenilworth, N. J.
PRICE - 25 CENTS

CRANFORD FIRE ENGINES, 1924. Standing in front of the 1909 firehouse on North Avenue East from left to right were paid firemen Samuel Cobb, Theodore C. Chamberlain, Engineer Collins, Chief William Tunison, and George Meyers. The three drivers are, from left to right, Charles Wesighan, Bernard Doyle (later chief), and Howard Shindler.

LOOKING SOUTH ALONG UNION AVENUE, NOVEMBER 1924. The Cranford Hotel is in the distance on the left, and today's Eastman Plaza would be on the right. The shot was taken from the center of the intersection of North Avenue and Union Avenue. Multiple signs at the railroad grade crossing warned of oncoming locomotives. One sign advised pedestrians to "Avoid Danger, Do Not Cross Tracks, Use the Subway" (a tunnel beneath the tracks).

LOOKING WEST DOWN NORTH AVENUE EAST, DECEMBER 1924. Railroad tracks came within 20 feet of the road at this time, as can be seen by the cars on the left, or south side of the avenue. The view looks toward Cranford's central business district. Railroad marshalling yards and a planing mill occupied the area between North Avenue East and South Avenue East.

"THE SPIRIT OF '76" IN '26. Cleveland School (Cleveland Plaza today) eighth graders presented this graduation play in the spring of 1926. Standing to the right of his magnificently costumed students was Principal Ray Clement. Note the shaggy pooch in front of Mr. Clement. One wonders which role called for a canine.

SIGNS OF THE TIMES, 25 NORTH AVENUE E., *c.* 1927. Motorists heading east on North Avenue East could not help but be distracted by this bold promotion. The Blakeslee and Blakeslee concern sold real estate and insured "everything but tomorrow." C.E. Blakeslee was also proprietor of The Paint Store, the brick-front shop to the right of the telephone pole.

THE CRANFORD GARAGE, *c.* 1927. The "Garage That Is Never Closed" was located at 31 North Avenue East, between the Blakeslee building (see above) and the Cranford fire house (on the right). Proprietor H.M. Hummer pumped gas, sold Goodyear and Horseshoe tires, and ran the local Chevrolet showroom in his garage.

DOWNTOWN IMPROVEMENTS AT THE PLAZA, FEBRUARY 12, 1927. This view of North Avenue West at Miln Street, showing tremendous change, was taken four and a half years after the photograph on p. 78. Most of the trees were gone. The road was paved and parking had been added. Stern's New Cranford Theater was in place on the right. The *Chronicle* building was gone, allowing us to see the tall smoke stack of the Public Service trolley power house. Shops along Eastman Street at this time included the Wo Lee Laundry, Nathan's Variety Store, The Plaza Grocer, The Collins Shop, a delicatessen-lunchroom, and Dr. Kahler Shoes.

UNION AVENUE SOUTH, NOVEMBER 22, 1927. This view looks south from the trolley tracks at the intersection with South Avenue. In the 1920s the area was a grocery corner. The building on the left housed a fruit and vegetable market where Perrotti's Meat Market is today. On the right corner was a small meat and poultry market and The Eagle Grocery Company (the Office Restaurant today).

OFFICE OF THE
GRAND DRAGON
KNIGHTS *of the* KU KLUX KLAN
REALM OF NEW JERSEY
SPECIAL BULLETIN

| Vol. 2 | Belmar, New Jersey, July 1, 1927, AK-LXI | No. |

First Annual State Celebration

AND

Third Anniversary

OF THE

AMERICAN KRUSADERS

WILL BE HELD ON

Saturday, July 16th, 1927

AT UPSLAR COLLEGE GROUNDS

Kenilworth, N. J.

DAY AND NIGHT

Klansmen it is more than a duty, it is an honor, to be of assistance to our allies the American Krusaders. Let us all turn out to this, their *First State Celebration.* The American Krusaders are always present in full force at every Klan Celebration. NOW let us show our appreciation by attending their first large event 100 per cent.

A LARGE PROGRAM OF DAY AND NIGHT EVENTS.

FIREWORKS - - MUSIC - - SPEAKERS - - CEREMONIES - - EATS

KOME ONE, KOME ALL. TO THE KRUSADERS KALL.

THE KLAN IN KENILWORTH, JULY 1927. Arthur H. Bell, Grand Dragon of the Realm of New Jersey, issued this "Special Bulletin" to advise klansmen of a celebration to be held on the grounds of Upsala College (misspelled "Upslar") in Kenilworth on July 16, 1927. The Klan was active in Kenilworth, Cranford, and Roselle, as indeed it was throughout the country in the Roaring Twenties. This four-page bulletin contained much against the "wet Governor" of New York, Al Smith, "the Pope's hope for the Presidency."

DOWNTOWN CRANFORD LAMPOONED, 1928. Cartoonist "Darsh" pictured the unstoppable Lion-drawn "Rotary Wagon" in downtown Cranford after a much-ballyhooed Lions-Rotary baseball game. The Rotary swamped the Lions Club 16 to 8. In the cartoon, local businesses and prominent businessmen were depicted as either Rotary or Lions adherents.

UNION-WALNUT AVENUE GRADE CROSSING, 1928. This tranquil view of the town's busiest grade crossing belies its notoriety as the site of so many motorist and pedestrian deaths over the years. As early as 1913 the six sets of tracks carried a total of 274 trains a day. The local newspaper said, "Track laborers, vagrants and prominent citizens of the town alike met their death through the confusion surrounding the poorly guarded crossings."

RAISING THE GRADE AT THE FOOT OF EASTMAN STREET, NOVEMBER 30, 1928. Concrete footings were being poured in order to elevate the railroad grade crossing. The building is the Miller block, still standing today. Stores along the street included a news and magazine store, Peltier the Tailor, F. Massa Dry Goods, The Model Bakery, Venice Shoe Repairing, Hummer Tires, and J.F. Doremus Groceries.

GOING, GOING, ALMOST GONE! 1929. Thirty-five years of controversy ended in April 1926, when the State Board of Public Utilities ordered the Central Railroad of New Jersey to eliminate the grade crossings at Lincoln and Union Avenues. Work was to begin by April 1, 1927, and be completed within three years. By August 1929, the first part of track elevation was nearly finished, as seen here. In January 1930, the project was completed, permanently altering the face of Cranford.

THE "EL," 1929. The construction of the Jersey Central's new "el" through downtown Cranford was nearing completion when this photograph was taken, looking north from Walnut Avenue. Some workmen and construction equipment are visible at left. The sign in the middle of the roadway said "Go Slow and Keep to Right." The dog appeared to be following both directives.

A SOUTHSIDE LANDMARK, ABOUT 1929. Four concrete coal-storage silos in the yards of the Reel-Strong Coal Company at Lexington Avenue and the railroad were the tallest structures built in Cranford up to that time. In addition to an American flag, the roof of the silos bore a huge painted arrow, visible only from the air, pointing to the word "Cranford." The silos held Lehigh Valley Black Diamond Coal. They were demolished in 1972/73.

LINING UP ON NORTH AVENUE, 1929. If there is one image of the Great Depression that comes to mind, it is lines. People by the thousands were seen in bread lines, soup lines, and employment lines. The line waiting to enter the Heins Real Estate office (a few doors down from the Cranford Diner) in this picture, however, is merely waiting to make last minute renewals of driver's licenses. Note the police officer, a young lady, and sailor on the steps. Is there a story here?

Six
Making Ends Meet
1930-1939

THE TRESTLE AND THE MILLER BLOCK, OCTOBER 27, 1930. The recently completed Jersey Central overpass was in place when this view was taken looking west from the foot of Eastman Street. Shops in the Miller Block (the first building) and adjacent buildings included, from left to right, E.L. Harris Newsdealer, Peltier the Tailor, F. Massa Dry Goods, The Model Bakery, Venice Shoe Repairing, and J.F. Doremus Grocer.

NORTHWEST CORNER, SOUTH AND WALNUT AVENUES, OCTOBER 27, 1930.
Standing next to the Cranford Hotel, this building housed Diamond's Confectionary and an
apparel store. A sign on the South Avenue side advised that Diamond's was "the only place in
Cranford selling Horton's Ice Cream." Later, in the 1950s, this cigar and candy store was famed
among Cranford youngsters as "Red's."

THE JERSEY CENTRAL OVERPASS, OCTOBER 27, 1930. Work had recently been
completed on the overpass when this photograph was taken. The view looks north from the
center of Walnut Avenue. The Cranford Hotel is on the left, serving as home to several retail
and professional businesses at that time. The closest automobile on the right was the delivery
car for the Progress Cleaners & Tailors at 5 Walnut Avenue.

NORTH AVENUE, DECEMBER 10, 1930. The downtown was just starting to come to life in this photograph taken on an early morning in December. Among the businesses in the Cranford Trust Company Building on the left were the Robbins and Allison Furniture Store and the Hathaway Pharmacy. In later years, the parking areas on the right became Eastman Plaza and Warner Plaza. The view was taken from atop a building on Eastman Street, looking down North Avenue.

CRANFORD'S FLYING DAYS. Yes, Cranford had its own airport! Located at the intersection of Walnut Avenue and Raritan Road (later the site of the Hyatt Bearings plant, now gone), it was not much more than an open field. The "airport" was operated by the Cranford Air Service, which flew a Ford Tri-Motor from the site. This May 1931 ad featured "Passenger Hopping" at only $1 per hop.

FLY IN SAFETY

—AT—

CRANFORD AIRPORT

Licensed Planes — Licensed Pilots

PASSENGER HOPPING $1

STUDENT INSTRUCTION

SPECIAL CHARTERED TRIPS ANYWHERE

PRICES QUOTED ON REQUEST

CRANFORD AIR SERVICE

C. R. Silkman — Matthew Seleski

Tel. CRanford 6-1303

Walnut Avenue and Raritan Road
Cranford, N. J.

FRANKENSTEIN COMES TO CRANFORD, JANUARY 28, 1932. The movies were the only big business to flourish in the Depression. Frankenstein, with Boris Karloff as the monster, became the most famous horror film ever made. The movie came to Cranford for a three-day run. The *Citizen and Chronicle* devoted nearly half a page to a photograph and story on the newly released film. Indeed, movie ads for area theaters constituted a high percentage of all advertising in the paper.

BIG GUNS, 1934. The Cranford High School Rifle Club looked like they meant business in this era of Bonnie and Clyde. At the front entrance of the high school (Cleveland School) were sponsor Frank Schoenwisner (top, center) with Virginia Barnes, Claribel Frew, Ruth Morris, William Dengler, Olendo DiFabio, William Fredericks, Harry Schork, Robert Harris, James Hollowell, Warner Lansing, and George "Ostrich" Osterheldt Jr. The club practiced in the local Methodist church.

SENIOR PLAY, 1934. Cranford High School seniors staged A.A. Milne's three-act play, *The Ivory Door*, on March 23-24, 1934, in Cleveland School. In this scene Perivale, played by Hobart Parsons, dealt with members of his authentically costumed court.

A. M.																	A. M.
	1	2	3	4	5	6	7	8	9	10	11	12	13	14	15	16	
P. M.																	P. M.

JAN.	STATE OF NEW JERSEY EMERGENCY RELIEF ADMINISTRATION OF UNION COUNTY	JULY
FEB.	**WORK CARD**	AUG.
MAR.		SEPT.
APR.	Dear Sir: Reg. No._____ You will report for ____ Days Work on_____	OCT.
MAY	_____ A. M.	NOV.
JUNE	at_____ **BRING THIS CARD WITH YOU** HENRY G. NULTON, County Director	DEC.

A. M.																A. M.
	17	18	19	20	21	22	23	24	25	26	27	28	29	30	31	
P. M.																P. M.

DEPRESSION-ERA WORK CARD, c. 1935. Many Cranford residents were lucky to find work, no matter where it came from. This card, issued by the New Jersey Emergency Relief Administration in Union County, allowed a registered worker to report for a specified number of days of government-supplied work at designated sites.

A FIREMAN'S WORK IS NEVER DONE, c. 1935. Cranford fireman Bernard Doyle was tightening a hose valve when this snapshot was taken at a fire in the thirties. "Beanie" Doyle was only the fifth paid man when he joined the department at age nineteen in 1923. He later served as chief, from 1957 to 1965.

94

THE LAST RUN, SEPTEMBER 14, 1935. Electric trolley car no. 2225 (Union line no. 49) was photographed coming into Cranford on its last day of operation. The scene is South Avenue West at the Garwood-Cranford border.

A BELOVED PHYSICIAN, 1935. Pediatrician Dr. Carl G. Hanson (1904-1980) opened an office in Cranford in 1934 and over succeeding decades provided care for hundreds of Cranford children. Dr. Hanson was a nationally recognized researcher in the field of strep throat. His former home and office at 38 Springfield Avenue is today a community building and headquarters of the Cranford Historical Society.

CONSTRUCTION OF THE NEW CRANFORD POST OFFICE, AUGUST 6, 1935. The foundation and basement walls of the new post office were progressing nicely when this photograph was taken on a warm summer day. In the background is the pennant-bedecked Cranford Theater, with a candy shop on the left and the Theater Diner and Lunchroom on the right. A used-car lot is to the extreme right.

POST OFFICE DEDICATION, APRIL 11, 1936. Five hundred spectators and guests gathered for the mid-Depression dedication of the township's new $71,000 post office. Accepting the building for the federal government that day, Assistant Postmaster General Clinton Eilenberger reminded the largely Republican crowd that Franklin D. Roosevelt was at the helm of the ship of state, which was "holding up well and will not go on the rocks," despite what was being said in some quarters.

A DOWNTOWN CRANFORD LANDMARK BUSINESS, 1936. In 1923 twelve-year old John E. Allen became a printer when he established a backyard print shop at his home in Cleveland, Ohio. In 1931 he and John Kasten established the A & K Printing Company in Cranford, and the next year it became the Allen Printing Company. The company and its building (purchased in 1936) at 41 North Avenue East were fixtures in downtown Cranford for fifty-three years, until sold in 1989. In this 1936 photograph are, left to right, John E. Allen, Robert A.Miskelly, and Leo Panewicz.

RURAL DIETZ STREET, AUGUST 1937. Much of Cranford was open countryside as late as the 1930s. This view looks east toward Roselle along Dietz Street between Bryant and Ludlow Avenues. Dietz Street recently had been "improved" by the addition of crushed stone. Many streets in Cranford were improved at this time by the federal government's Works Progress Administration (WPA). Local road projects were required to have a "high social value . . . to give employment to persons on the relief roles." Cranford's Road Committee Chairman reported that "every qualified worker in Cranford was given employment."

RAY A. CLEMENT, CHS PRINCIPAL. Although a native of New Hampshire, Clement (1887-1972) lived in Cranford for fifty years, and he became one of the high school's longest-serving and most popular principals. He started as high school (Cleveland School) principal in 1922 and became the first principal of the new high school in 1938, retiring from the school system in 1949. Active in a number of community groups, Clement was president of the Cranford Dramatic Club and a trustee of the Cranford Historical Society.

CRANFORD HIGH SCHOOL, WEST END PLACE. Dedicated on January 3, 1938, as a six-year high school, CHS graduated its first class (transferred from Cleveland School) in June of the same year. The forty-nine-classroom building cost $850,000, nearly half the amount coming from the New Deal's Public Works Administration. The extensive growth of hedges (gone today) in front of the school was known as the "Green Trolley." Upperclassmen often gave freshmen a free ride in it.

98

CARLANGELO MASSA RELAXING, 1938. Born in the small village of Monte Ferrante, Italy, Carl Massa (1885-1938) came to the U.S. in 1901 and joined the Cranford Police Department fifteen years later. In 1933 Massa was appointed the department's third chief of police, a position he held until his death. Powerfully built, square-jawed, and absolutely fearless, he was a storybook cop. Off duty he enjoyed cigars and fishing.

SUPERIOR OFFICERS AND MOBILE EQUIPMENT, 1938. Cranford's police chief and his senior officers posed proudly with patrol cars no.'s. 1, 2, and 3, and the department's Harley-Davidson motorcycle. From left to right were Sgt. Lawrence Bonnell Sr., Sgt. Edward Metzner, Chief Carl Massa, Lt. William Fischer, and Sgt. George Rosendale.

SPRUCE STREET, MAY 1939. In this view looking north from West End Place, cars belonging to Cranford High School teachers and students lined Spruce Street, just as they do today. Cranford's quaint concrete obelisk street signs, as seen in this picture, originally had letter tiles spelling out the street name.

STATION PLAZA AND DOWNTOWN, ABOUT 1939. The intersection of North Union and North Avenues is shown in this postcard view. The Reel-Strong Coal Company office was on the corner to the left, and the Public Service sign above the old trolley power house on South Avenue can be seen in the distance on the right. The road surface was composed of large slabs of asphaltic concrete.

Seven

The Homefront and Post-War Years 1940-1949

ENGLISH VILLAGE, 1940. Shown here is an architect's rendering of the apartment complex built on the 120,000 square-foot site of the Thomas Sperry estate. Fronting on Clarement Place and Prospect and Casino Avenues, the three- and four-story apartment groups boasted a 250-foot-long landscaped central court. Sperry's original decorative iron fence and most of the estate's fine trees were preserved.

THE FIRST TO GO, NOVEMBER 26, 1940. Local civic officials and Selective Service Board No. 5 posed in the Cranford Casino at a send-off dinner for the first seven inductees drawn from the Cranford district (Cranford, Garwood, Clark). All seven young men, ages eighteen to twenty-two, actually volunteered before their numbers were called. The seven were (front row, five on left and two on right) W.R. Clarkson, Thomas Criscuola, Harley Ferrel, Ernest Sanders and Lewis Sanders (brothers), John Bobusky, and Walter Sternenberg. By passing the hat that evening, the sums of $21 and $15 were put aside to await the first of the seven to obtain sergeant's and corporal's stripes, respectively. Selective Service Board chairman Linford Hazzard pointed out that the sergeant's award was a month's pay. Each man that evening was given a wrist watch, flashlight, pocket knife, carton of cigarettes, toothbrush, and kit of toilet articles. By June of 1941 (six months before Pearl Harbor) the Cranford district had to send a quota of 138 draftees or volunteers into the armed forces.

NUMBER PLEASE! 1940. Lt. George Rosendale (left) and Patrolman Anton Kovacs checked in with headquarters from a police and fire call-box "security pedestal." Rosendale, who spent forty-three years on the police force, gained local fame in 1927 when, as a patrolman, he leaped from a moving car onto the back of a runaway horse and brought the galloping animal to a halt.

SEARS-BUILT, 1941. In 1940 Sears, Roebuck & Company began a housing development in the treeless fields of Osceola Farms in south Cranford. Before the war brought an end to home construction, 180 "Sears houses" lined the winding drives between Raritan Road and the Rahway River. The new owners formed their own civic association and called their community "Sunny Acres." The house shown here, at 9 Iroquois Road, was built in 1941 and purchased by Wesley Philo, later mayor and township clerk in Cranford.

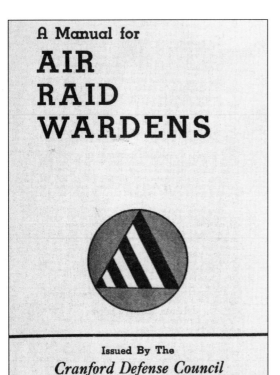

A Manual for

AIR RAID WARDENS

Issued By The

Cranford Defense Council

Cranford, N. J.   January, 1942

CRANFORD AIR RAID WARDEN MANUAL, 1942. Fear of air attack was very real in the first two years of World War II. Cranford was divided into ten zones, each headed by a zone warden who reported to the town's chief air raid warden. In the event of an attack, block wardens were responsible for stopping vehicular traffic, clearing the street of people, and ensuring that a complete blackout was in effect. Wardens were also charged with assessing post-attack damage and injuries, but of course it never came to that.

LT. ROGER S. NORTON JR. (1919-1943). Lt. Norton was the first CHS graduate (Class of '36) to lose his life in World War II. An honor student at the University of Michigan, he left in his junior year to enter the navy as an air cadet. As a member of the neutrality patrol force in the North Atlantic in 1941, he participated in the successful search for the German battleship *Bismarck*. In 1942 he served as a pilot for Admiral Nimitz. Returning from a rescue mission in the South Pacific on January 1, 1943, his PBY flying boat crashed while attempting a landing in Guadalcanal's Lunga Point harbor. Roger Norton Place is named for him.

FIREMAN 1/C ROBERT GRECO, 1943. Bob Greco joined the navy in May 1943, with Joseph Griffin and James Roberts, friends from Cranford. Serving on the USS *Canberra* in the Pacific, they went through eighteen engagements together. On Friday the 13th, October 1944, their ship was hit by a Japanese aerial torpedo, and Roberts was one of twenty-three men killed. Later, Greco and Griffin were amazed to read in a *Citizen and Chronicle* sent from home that another local man, Ensign Howard Goodman, had also been killed in the attack. Goodman had been aboard the ship only three weeks, and neither Greco nor Griffin knew he was from their hometown.

HELPING TO WIN THE WAR, 1943. Twenty-year-old Laura Hogan of 9 Wall Street in Cranford received a $1,000 war bond from Philip Baugh, plant manager at the Eastern Aircraft Division of the General Motors Corporation in Linden. She was the first woman employee at General Motors to win the highest award possible for a time-saving production suggestion she made. The award was made even more poignant because some time earlier, her fiance, a navy pilot, was killed in combat over Makin Island in the Pacific.

A.E. DIMMICK, 1ST LT. - 4

DEDICATION OF THE CRANFORD SERVICE FLAG, FEBRUARY 22, 1943. Presented by the Lion's Club, Cranford's service flag hung above the foot of Alden Street, around the corner from the municipal offices on North Avenue. Three gold stars within a circle of twelve blue stars represented the three Cranford servicemen who had lost their lives in the war up until that time. In accepting the flag, Mayor George Osterheldt attacked "chiseling patriots" and those at home who complained of the small sacrifices they were called upon to make.

1ST LT. ALLEN E. DIMMICK. Born in Westfield, Allen Dimmick was a 1936 CHS graduate and a 1941 Louisiana State University graduate. Commissioned in 1941, he was first an artillery instructor but later transferred to the Air Corps. A P-47 fighter pilot, the twenty-four-year old Dimmick was killed in action over Pas de Calais in France on January 21, 1944. At the time of his death, his brother Carl was a guest of the Germans at a prisoner-of-war camp 50 miles outside of Berlin.

CORPORAL DURHAM IN ENGLAND, 1944. Corporal Ferman Durham (back row, second from left), CHS class of '40, served in the Army Medical Corps and was assigned to the 182nd General Hospital in England. This was one of a handful of racially integrated units in the segregated armed forces of the day. Another Cranford soldier, James Franklin, served in the same unit. Integration only went so far, however. Although the men worked and played ball together, their barracks were segregated. Here, some members of the hospital's softball team posed for a picture after a game at Derby, England.

A CHANCE MEETING, JUNE 9, 1944. Three Cranford servicemen had an unexpected reunion in wartime Foggia, Italy. From left to right, Tech. Sgt. Vincent Dooley, Flight Officer Alan Cooper, and Staff Sgt. Alfred Fricke, each a member of a different unit, met by accident. None had known of the presence of the others. Cooper and Fricke had been schoolmates and sang in the Trinity Episcopal Church Boys' Choir.

ONCE A MARINE, ALWAYS A MARINE, 1944. Charles F. Hansel served in two world wars as a member of the U.S. Marine Corps. "Cap" came to Cranford in 1906 at the age of thirteen. In World War I he joined the marines and rose from private to first lieutenant. In World War II, he again volunteered and became a major in marine aviation, serving as a headquarters squad commander on Bougainville. Hansel was also a well-known deep-water yachtsman. In February 1954, he was lost in a storm at sea while piloting his yacht *Capella* from Palm Beach to Nassau, Bahamas.

A CRANFORD "G.I. JOE," FEBRUARY 22, 1945. T/4 Robert Hume took a moment to read mail from home while at a forward message center in the Mt. Belvedere area of Italy. Hume was a radio operator in Headquarters Co., 2nd Battalion, 85th Mountain Infantry, 10th Mtn. Division, in the Fifth Army.

CRANFORD'S FIGHTING FAMILY. Augustine D'Alessandris had seven brothers and a sister, children of Mr. and Mrs. Natale D'Alessandris. "Augie" graduated from Cranford High in 1940 and enlisted in the army in June 1942. Two years later he participated in the D-Day Invasion of Normandy and was killed in action on June 23, 1944. His brothers Alfred, Albert, and Louis were also in the army. Alfred, a gunner aboard a B-17 Flying Fortress, was a prisoner-of-war in Germany for thirteen months. Another brother, Ralph, was severely injured while serving in the merchant marine.

RED CROSS OVERSEAS, AUGUST 1945. Cranford's Elsie P. Hansel (right) joined her sister Red Cross staff assistants in posing around an anti-aircraft gun while crossing the Atlantic. Miss Hansel was headed for Nice, France, where she worked in a recreation-rehabilitation center for war-weary G.I.'s. She later wrote home that "I have learned invaluable things about tolerance, sacrifice, sincerity . . . mere words before, now have taken a real meaning written in the blood of young Americans."

LT. AND MRS. VINCENT SARNOWSKI, DECEMBER 29, 1945. Large numbers of servicemen married just before going overseas and an equally large number married upon their return. Here, Lt. Vincent Sarnowski (4th Tank Group) and his bride, the former Bernice Doyle, come down the aisle at St. John's R.C. Church in Orange. Vince, who had spent four years overseas, returned to his teaching job in Cranford, where he later became a principal and superintendent of schools.

A FUTURE MAYOR, HOME FROM INDIA, 1946. Sporting five six-month overseas service stripes on his sleeve, Army Air Corps Lt. Ira Dorian was glad to be home. A graduate of Princeton University and Harvard Law School, he enlisted in 1942 and later received a direct commission. Lt. Dorian served in the CBI (China-Burma-India) Theater Judge Advocate General's Department in New Delhi and Calcutta. Dorian was Cranford's mayor in 1959 and 1960.

THE CRANFORD HIGH SCHOOL BAND, 1946. The capped and caped high school marching band strode along North Avenue East in Cranford's October 12, 1946, "Welcome Home Parade" for servicemen and women. The parade brought out 1,500 marchers and 15,000 onlookers. Businesses that can be seen in the background include the Cranford Savings & Loan Association, Reel-Strong Coal Company, McPherson Real Estate, Cranford Piano Company, and the Cranford Diner.

THERE IS A TOLL ROAD IN YOUR FUTURE, 1946. On November 8, 1946, Mayor George E. Osterheldt (left), State Senator Herbert Pascoe (center), and Cranford Police Commissioner J. Edward Wolf posed with the shovel used to break ground at the town line for the new Route 4, N.J. Parkway. The great north-south artery later became the Garden State Parkway.

MEMORIAL FIELD, 1948. This aerial view shows Memorial Field just before its official dedication. The row of houses on the left are on Myrtle Avenue. Perhaps the most striking aspect of the landscape in this pre-Parkway era was the openness, both in Cranford (upper left) and in Roselle (upper right).

MEMORIAL FIELD DEDICATION, JULY 5, 1948. Boy Scouts, police, rotary, American Legion, V.F.W., and other organizations trooped the colors past Mayor George Osterheldt and dignitaries in the reviewing stand. An inaugural baseball game and two softball games began playing while the dedication ceremony was taking place. Note the sound car in the foreground.

TAKING THE OATH, MARCH 1949. Five new Cranford patrolmen were sworn in by Police Commissioner J. Edward Wolf (center, holding bible) in front of the sergeant's desk at police headquarters. From left to right were Township Clerk J.W. Coffee, Paul Johnson, Alfred Oram, Commissioner Wolfe, Ralph J. Koury, Michael Fedroff, and John J. Herzer.

WALNUT AVENUE, JULY 1949. This view looks south along Walnut from the vantage point of the railroad trestle. Some of the businesses along the left (east) side of the avenue were a barbershop, Barnett's Wines and Liquors, Peter Pan Dry Cleaners, and Kings Superette. On the right (west) side were the old Cranford Hotel, Paramount Cleaners, Ed's Stationary & Soda, Scher's Drugs, another liquor store, and the Cranford Delicatessen.

SHIRTSLEEVE PARADE, AUGUST 1949. There certainly was no prescribed uniform of the day for these intrepid marchers from Newell Rodney Fiske Post No. 335 of the Veterans of Foreign Wars. Due to the fierce August heat some of the marchers wore only an undershirt with military trousers. The occasion was the dedication and ground breaking for the new VFW home at 479 South Avenue East.

CRANFORD'S LEADING SUFFRAGIST, IN 1949. Elizabeth Miller Bates (b. 1879) came to Cranford as a child in 1890. In addition to serving forty-five years in the Red Cross, she fought for women's right to vote. In 1912 she was a founder of the Equal Franchise League in Cranford. She explained that she had been a poll watcher when an illiterate drunk appeared and put his "X" on the ballot. It made her blood boil to think that he could vote and she could not. Mrs. Bates died in 1980 at the age of 101.

Eight
The Fabulous Fifties
1950-1960

THE LIBERTY BELL IN CRANFORD, JUNE 2, 1950. A 2,000-pound replica Liberty Bell, one of fifty-two cast in France, made its appearance at Cranford schools to promote the sale of U.S. savings bonds. Gathered by the bell were (left to right) CPD Lt. Lester Powell, William Jones (local VFW commander), Robert E. Crane (president of the Cranford Trust Co), Charles Ray (editor of the *Citizen and Chronicle*), Supervising Principal Dr. Howard Best, Postmaster Arthur Metz, Michael Davis (commander of the American Legion post), and a state trooper escort.

SWITCHER AT THE ROUNDHOUSE, *c.* 1950. This type of 0-6-0 switcher locomotive, seen outside the Jersey Central's roundhouse on South Avenue, was a familiar sight in Cranford when steam still ruled the rails. The old roundhouse, since modified, is now home to the township's department of public works.

POLICE EXHIBIT, MacCONNELL PARK, JUNE 9, 1950. Young boys flocked to the CPD display of radios, firearms, and safety equipment at this annual Cranford Day event in the park. Lt. Lester Powell and Chief William Fischer were in attendance. The day included commercial and civic displays, boxing matches, and a block dance.

"PARAMOUNT GARDENS," 1950. These garden apartments opened in September of 1950. The complex is located at 12-18 Riverside Drive, at the corner of Prospect Avenue, the former site of "The Riverside," a fashionable boarding house. Today, the "Paramount" is known as the "Riverside Garden Apartments."

NORTH AVENUE SERVICE STATION, OCTOBER 25, 1950. Looking across North Avenue East we see Bibby's Coach and Four Restaurant (right). The c. 1890 tenements next to the restaurant are long since gone. An NBC Bread van can be seen in the street. The Gulf station sold two grades of gasoline at this time: Good Gulf at 18.9¢ a gallon and No-Nox at 20.9¢ per gallon.

PRESBYTERIAN CHURCH MANSE, 1950. A familiar sight on Springfield Avenue was the second manse of the First Presbyterian Church. It was built in 1871 following completion of the original church edifice on this property. The manse was demolished in July 1950, to make way for a new $150,000 church school building.

AMERICAN-LaFRANCE LADDER TRUCK IN 1950. This old fire engine is seen in front of the fire house (1909-1980) on North Avenue East. The truck had discarded its wooden-spoked wheels and hard-rubber tires for a more modern look, but it still had mechanical brakes—and it steered from the right side. In the left foreground is the King's Food Mart, later replaced by an indoor-golf putting range.

SERVICE WITH A SMILE, c. 1950. Attendants wearing caps and coveralls worked at O'Brien's Esso Service on the corner of North Avenue West and Orchard Street. Gasoline was only 23¢ a gallon at this "beehive of modern service station activity."

OFFICER CARUSO AT THE READY, c. 1950. Officer Frank Caruso is seen here with radio car no. 2. He spent thirty years in the department, retiring in 1958. Known as "Chief" because of his refusal of a promotion that did not make him chief, Caruso was famed for sometimes wearing a scarf, a holdover from his days as a motorcycle patrolman.

POST OFFICE PLAZA, ABOUT 1951. This view, taken from in front of the post office on Miln Street, looks east along North Avenue West to its junction with Eastman Street. On the left along Eastman, Fern's Furniture & Appliances and a Philco appliance store on the corner can be seen. On the right, along North Avenue, are Leshner's Fabric Center, Cranford Cycle Company, a soda fountain-luncheonette, and the 1,212-seat Cranford Theater.

CRANFORD'S LONGTIME MAYOR, 1951. No other mayor of the township comes close to the record—eighteen years served between 1933 and 1951—held by George E. Osterheldt (1888-1967). Born in Darby, Pennsylvania, he lived in Cranford thirty-four years. His tenure as mayor spanned the Great Depression, World War II, the post-war years, and the Korean conflict.

MR. CRANFORD, 1951. Born in Cranford in 1867, Nathaniel R. Foster (d. 1952) was known as the town's oldest commuter, having taken the Jersey Central for sixty-seven years. Foster was township clerk, chairman of the police committee, president of the historical society, and president of the Cranford Trust Company. "Nat" was Cranford's "grand old man," famed for chartering entire trains to take local children on outings to the Jersey Shore.

NORTH AVENUE, 1951. Looking west from in front of the Coach and Four Restaurant, we see Eastman Street in the distance. On the right on North Avenue, sandwiched between a piano store and the Cranford Pet Shop, is the Cranford Diner. Above and to the rear of the diner was the law office of Ira D. Dorian, later mayor of Cranford.

THE SILVER WHISTLE, DECEMBER 7-8, 1951. The entire cast of the Cranford Dramatic Club's production of The Silver Whistle appeared together on stage. Real-life Cranford patrolman George Ward (third from left) was at home in the role of a police officer.

THE TOWNSHIP COMMITTEE IN SESSION, JANUARY 1, 1952. The first meeting of the new year was brought to order by Mayor (Admiral) Emory D. Stanley (with gavel, at center). On the dais, from left to right, were Clarence Fritz, Fred Anderson, Mayor Stanley, J. Walter Coffee, and James Duffy. At the press table were reporter Jim Sutter (left) and *Citizen and Chronicle* publisher Charles Ray. Township offices and the council chamber were located at this time in the small commercial office building on North Avenue East near the foot of Alden Street.

ADMIRAL ON THE AIR, 1952. WOR radio in New York City conducted a community service broadcast interview with Cranford Mayor Admiral Emory D. Stanley (U.S.N., retired; see above). Interviewing the admiral were radio personalities Pat Barnes (left), "the world's most popular announcer," and his daughter, Barbara. Stanley was wearing an "Ike" pin (it was only a few days before the presidential election) and a World War II "ruptured duck" discharge pin in his lapel.

The plaque reads:

CHARLES ABBOTT HARKER, JR.

FIRST LIEUTENANT, USAF
F-84 PILOT

311TH FIGHTER-BOMBER SQ.,
56TH FIGHTER-BOMBER GP

b. SEPTEMBER 1, 1930, BAYONNE, NJ · M.I.A. MAY 4, 1953 OVER NORTH KOREA
GRADUATE, CRANFORD HIGH SCHOOL 1948

IN 1993, FORTY YEARS AFTER THE KOREAN WAR, THE UNITED STATES GOVERNMENT PRESENTED
EVIDENCE TO THE RUSSIAN GOVERNMENT THAT HUNDREDS OF AMERICAN PRISONERS WERE
SECRETLY TRANSPORTED TO THE SOVIET UNION AND NEVER HEARD FROM AGAIN. CHARLES HARKER
IS LISTED AMONG THOSE LIKELY TO HAVE BEEN RETAINED BY THE SOVIETS

"I have slipped the surly bonds of earth,
danced the skies on laughter - silvered wings
and touched the face of God"   - J. Magee

DEDICATED IN HONOR AND REMEMBRANCE OF LT. HARKER
AND ALL M.I.A.'s BY HIS CLASSMATES,
CRANFORD HIGH SCHOOL CLASS OF 1948 · APRIL 30, 1994

MISSING IN ACTION. The Korean conflict of 1950-1953 was America's forgotten war. Air Force 1st Lt. Charles A. Harker Jr. of Arbor Street in Cranford was an F-84 fighter-bomber pilot. He disappeared over Sinanju, North Korea, on May 4, 1953, while on a night intruder mission. Evidence discovered forty years later indicated that he had been captured and transported to the Soviet Union, never to be heard from again. On April 30, 1994, Harker's classmates from the Cranford High School Class of 1948 dedicated this monument in his honor in Memorial Park.

THE FIRST AID SQUAD'S FIRST AMBULANCE. Organized in May of 1953, the Cranford First Aid Squad took over the old municipal ambulance the following November. The vehicle was a 1941 Packard, brought to Cranford from Boston in 1942. It was kept in service with the squad until 1957. That is Al Smith by the open door of the ambulance.

"STAN THE MAN" AND FRIENDS, CRANFORD BOYS CAMP, *c.* 1953. Stanley Grayson (front row, third from right), director of the camp from 1948 to 1954, posed with the cook and counselors on the dock at Silver Lake. Born Stanley Gurzynski in Catasaqua, Pennsylvania, Stan was a legendary CHS football coach and physical education teacher. He played in the first Sugar Bowl in the 1930s and later played semi-pro football for a Philadelphia Eagles farm team. A fifty-year Cranford resident, Stan died in January of 1996 at the age of eighty-three.

LOOK! UP IN THE SKY, *c.* 1954. Fear of Soviet atomic attack gripped America during the Cold War years, and volunteers took an active part in civil defense. Here, four members of Cranford's BSA Explorer Post 79 served as airplane spotters atop a building in Elizabeth. They were, from left, Fred Sickert, Al Gessler, Charles Turner, and Cling Munday.

"CRANFORD'S NO. 1 CITIZEN," 1956. Roderick W. Smith (1886-1972) came to Cranford as a child in 1893 and lived here for nearly eighty years. Few local organizations did not benefit from his participation, and he was particularly known for his scouting and historical society work. After he and his wife Vera lost their son, Roderick Jr., in World War II, Smith turned to the young people of Cranford. Rod found much pleasure in telling local children stories of his experiences at the turn of the century. This portrait of Smith was painted by Alice Crump in 1956.

CRANFORD'S WINNINGEST COACH, 1957. Georgia-born J. Seth Weekly (1895-1969) claimed American Indian ancestry. He could also claim an enviable record as the Cranford High School track, baseball, basketball, and football coach, retiring in 1958 after a twenty-nine-year career. In indoor-outdoor track alone, his teams compiled a record of 132 wins and 20 losses, and in 17 of 28 seasons his outdoor teams were undefeated. Cranford honored the coach in June of 1957 with a Weekly Day celebration, and the new high school track was dedicated as J. Seth Weekly Field.

REV. DR. BENJAMIN W.P. ALLEN.
An innovative clergyman, Benjamin Allen
(1890-1965) served as pastor of the First
Baptist Church on High Street from 1934 to
1965. During this time he introduced a
variety of imaginative programs. A Food Club
and a Coal Purchasing Club helped his
parishioners combat the shortages of the war
years. A Parish Development Association
assisted members in buying homes, and in
1944 the church founded a state-chartered
credit union, which by 1960 had processed
over $1,000,000 in loans.

UJC ON OPEN HOUSE DAY, JANUARY 17, 1960. The Nomahegan Building of Union
Junior College on Springfield Avenue, facing Nomahegan Park, presented a modern but stark
appearance when it first opened, surrounded by open fields of clay and mud. Previous homes for
UJC included Roselle High School (1933-1942) and Grant School in Cranford (1942-1960).

127

DICK TAKES THE MIKE, OCTOBER 4, 1960. Vice President Richard M. Nixon was the unsuccessful Republican presidential candidate (John F. Kennedy won) in 1960. Stopping in Cranford, Nixon made an unscheduled ten-minute speech standing on the trunk of his convertible, while Pat Nixon (right) pinned on a corsage. In the crowd on the left are Mayor Ira Dorian (glasses, head turned away from camera) and future mayor Wesley Philo (light suit, wearing Nixon button). Cranford went for Nixon, 8,059 to 5,064. The scene is North Avenue East in front of the Mayfair Super Market, adjacent to the old firehouse.

Well, so long! Come again soon!